Workers of the World Undermined

American Labor's Role in
U.S. Foreign Policy

Beth Sims

South End Press   Boston, MA

Copyright © 1992 Beth Sims

produced by the South End Press collective
manufactured in the U.S.A.
cover design by John Hawley
cover photo by Margaret Randall: banana workers in Nicaragua

Cataloging in Publication Data
Sims, Beth.
    Workers of the world undermined : American labor's role in U.S. foreign policy / Beth Sims. — 1st ed.
        p.   cm.
    Includes bibliographical references and index.
    ISBN 0-89608-430-2 : $30.00. — ISBN 0-89608-429-9 (pbk.) : $9.00 1. Trade-unions and foreign policy — United States. 2. AFL-CIO. I. Title.
HD6490.F582U617 1992   92-7004
322'.2'0973—dc20   CIP
South End Press, 116 St. Botolph Street, Boston MA 02115
        99 98 97 96 95 94 93 92   1 2 3 4 5 6 7 8 9

About the Resource Center:

The Inter-Hemispheric Education Resource Center is a private, nonprofit research and policy institute located in Albuquerque, New Mexico. Founded in 1979, the Resource Center produces books, policy reports, audiovisuals, and other educational materials about foreign policy, as well as sponsoring popular education projects. For more information and a catalog of publications, please write to the Resource Center, Box 4506, Albuquerque, New Mexico 87196.

Author profile:

Beth Sims is a research associate at the Resource Center. She is the author of *National Endowment for Democracy: A Foreign Policy Branch Gone Awry* (Resource Center, 1990) and a variety of articles on the foreign activities of U.S. private organizations.

Acknowledgments:

This study resulted from the contributions and encouragement of a number of individuals inside and outside the U.S. labor community. My thanks go first of all to Tom Barry and Debra Preusch, my friends and co-workers, for their prodding, feedback, advice, and support. Thanks too go to my editor Steve Chase and his colleagues at South End Press. I am also grateful to the following individuals for their criticisms, comments, and perspectives: Hobart Spalding, Jr., Dave Dyson, Charlie Kernaghan, Debi Duke, and many others in the AFL-CIO who asked me to respect their confidentiality. Despite the many contributions made by these individuals and others, the views and analysis should be considered exclusively my own.

The generous support of the J. Roderick MacArthur Foundation, Muste Institute, Dominican Sisters Poverty, Justice, and Peace Fund, National Community Funds, and Samuel Rubin Foundation made this project possible.

Dedication:

This book is lovingly dedicated to my mother, whose support for and acceptance of my often-controversial choices in life have given me the courage to keep growing and exploring this complicated world.

Table of Contents

Introduction

International labor solidarity has never been more essential than it is today. The world economic system is undergoing dramatic changes that are affecting the types of jobs people do and the conditions under which they do them. Businesses are growing larger, and many of the largest corporations have operations spanning the globe. Automation, the communications revolution, and new methods of subdividing the labor process are converting the world into a global factory. Workers on opposites sides of the earth, divided by barriers of language, culture, and relative privilege, are actually linked together in a common relationship.

As transnational corporations move lucrative operations to areas where labor is cheapest and where governmental protections are weakest, workers everywhere feel the downward tug. In the face of this ongoing restructuring of the global economy, led by transnational corporations and the financial institutions that back them, the working conditions, wages, and political power of all workers are, in the words of Jeremy Brecher and Tim Costello, being "harmonized downward" toward the level of the most impoverished and oppressed in the world today.[1] These economic changes have helped fuel a growing international crisis of poverty and oppression. In response, transnational labor solidarity and militancy are needed to spark a "harmonization upwards" of labor conditions throughout the world economy.

But such a task is not an easy one. Joe Gunn, president of the Texas AFL-CIO, described the dilemma:

> The "big picture" is this: wealthy capitalists are international in scope and run a global system; workers don't have a global system to protect themselves from such exploitation. The labor movement simply hasn't achieved the global organization necessary to defend workers everywhere.[2]

Yet Gunn's comment tells only part of the picture. Since the end of World War II, organized labor in the United States has aggressively

1

developed ties to the international labor community. Through the AFL-CIO and its four international arms—the Free Trade Union Institute, American Institute for Free Labor Development, African-American Labor Center, and Asian-American Free Labor Institute—the U.S. labor community has reached across the globe to join hands with foreign counterparts.[3] Along with the AFL-CIO's Department of International Affairs and the federation's European office, these institutes have sponsored numerous projects designed to strengthen their overseas allies. They have funded foreign unions, provided education and training, supplied technical assistance, developed agrarian unions, sponsored social service projects, conducted informational activities and visitor exchanges, and supported political action programs.

Although many of the individual programs sponsored by the AFL-CIO have helped foreign labor and even been sought by it, the overall foreign policy which is carried out by the AFL-CIO and its institutes often harms workers both in this country and overseas. Derived from the ideological biases of a select group of top labor bureaucrats—many of whom lack actual trade union experience—the resulting policies have stressed anticommunism at the expense of worker militancy. Simultaneously, these policies have affirmed the right of the United States to intervene in the affairs of other countries, whether through governmental or private actors.

In the process, foreign labor movements have been shaped to fit the needs of the United States government and business sector. Their capacity to develop independently of foreign intervention has been curtailed. Their most vigorous spokespeople have been undercut and co-opted. Left in the wake of AFL-CIO intervention are a collection of don't-rock-the-boat unions which often prove to be inadequate representatives of their own country's workers. They also serve as feeble allies for workers in developed countries hoping to unite in powerful global solidarity movements against corporate exploitation. Instead of advancing the cause of international worker solidarity, the AFL-CIO has undermined it. It has damaged the capacity of the world's workers to counter effectively the "harmonization downward" that is both hitting workers hard in the United States and sustaining the fierce oppression of workers in underdeveloped and developing countries.

The full scope of the AFL-CIO's international operations has never been adequately explored, although several important and insightful partial attempts have been made.[4] This book is an attempt to find answers to some difficult questions. How does the AFL-CIO conduct its operations overseas? What role do the international operations of the labor institutes play in the expansion of U.S. business and government influence around the world? What are the labor federation's ties to other private groups involved in the so-called "democracy-building" efforts which have become a major pillar of U.S. foreign policy? How extensive is the federation's alliance with Washington on overseas projects, and what motivates that partnership? Is the AFL-CIO an accountable institution? What projects do the institutes conduct overseas? What are the impacts of these projects on foreign labor?

Not much has been written on this topic, and no wonder. The labor network's complexity and shadowy nature make investigations of its international activities a mind-boggling task. The structural features of the network alone are daunting. The AFL-CIO has some 100 full-time professionals active in international affairs in the United States and in nearly 40 other countries.[5] *Business Week* described the federation's global operations as "labor's own version of the Central Intelligence Agency—a trade union network existing in all parts of the world, in all factions."[6]

To really grapple with the questions we ask in this report, therefore, one must divulge the secrets of four separate labor institutes, pull back the curtain on the inner sanctum of the AFL-CIO's foreign policy—the International Affairs Department—and scrutinize the projects and impacts of AFL-CIO operations in scores of countries with diverse histories, political structures, and economic systems.

Equally important, the exact configurations of the relationship between the labor federation and the U.S. government must be illuminated. But the visible ties that bind the two together—in terms of funding, policy and program selection, oversight mechanisms, and the like—only hint at a broader, more entangled relationship that originated in joint labor-intelligence operations during World War II. The details of that association are protected by all concerned.

Even in Congress, where the impulse for exposing labor's role in executive branch foreign policy might conceivably resonate, bipartisan support for the AFL-CIO's overseas operations stifles most attempts at scrutiny. Speaking of the AFL-CIO's government-funded foreign operations, a congressional staffer told us, "There are skeletons in the closet that the Democrats don't want to see fall out, any more than the Republicans do." Whether there is a "Bush or a Dukakis in the White House," the staffer continued, "they [Congress] won't open those closets."[7]

There is another formidable obstacle to uncovering the nature of the AFL-CIO's overseas activities. People who are in the best positions to know details of the labor federation's operations and decision-making process—trade unionists in particular—generally refuse to be cited on the record. As one progressive labor activist said in an interview, "It's like a Mafia out there. Nobody's talking." Many of the most insightful comments we heard about the federation, its relationship with the U.S. government, its impact overseas, and the manner and method of its decision-making were made to us only if we guaranteed the speaker's anonymity. In respect for the concerns of these unionists, their comments—unless otherwise indicated—are included in the text with a brief description of the roles they play in their unions, but without attribution.

Building Business Unionism

The labor federation describes its work as the support of "free" unions overseas. On the face of it, the AFL-CIO's definition of free unions is straightforward and unproblematic. The basic criteria the federation says it uses to identify such unions are their independence from government and company control and their commitment to pluralism and democratic procedures.[8] As described by the federation, "Authentic trade unions are not tools of the state, of political parties, or of employers. They are voluntary associations created by workers for mutual support, to give voice to their needs and to advance their interests—as *workers* define them."[9] In theory, they are democratically organized bodies that work diligently for workers' rights, improved working conditions, and livable wages.

In reality, however, the "free" trade unions supported by the AFL-CIO are those that are most receptive to U.S. economic and political influence in their countries and to the notions of "business unionism." This fact stems from the philosophy that drives both domestic and foreign policy in the labor federation. That philosophy rests upon an acceptance of capitalism and the relationships between workers, owners, and government that it produces. Labor and business, along with government, are seen not as inevitable opponents, but as potential partners in political and economic development. The prospect of this potential alliance inspires the conservative concept of business unionism. Described by one labor analyst as a "tacit alliance between the captains of industry and their labor lieutenants," it is this concept of unionism that the AFL-CIO exports to its international allies.[10]

Samuel Gompers, the first president of the American Federation of Labor (AFL) described this type of unionism as "trade unionism pure and simple." In this form of unionism, workers fight for the wages and benefits that the market will bear, and organizing takes place at the level of the factory, industrial sector, or confederations among sectors. But business unionism excludes the notion that workers form a class with widely shared characteristics. By emphasizing narrow, sectoral interests, business unionism tends to isolate groups of workers from one another. It likewise hampers the creation of coalitions with other sectors in society, such as environmental activists, or the homeless and unemployed.

Because workers and capitalists are idealized as partners in progress, there is no analysis of the fundamental relationships of capitalism that, by their nature, limit the advancement of most workers over the long run. Briefly, these relationships have two central features. Workers compete with other workers to sell their labor, and owners exploit those workers by undervaluing the true worth of their labor in order to make a profit. Business unionism does not recognize the existence of this fundamental exploitative relationship as the necessary motor of capitalist profit-making. Instead, it treats workers as members of sectoral interest groups that can be individually strengthened in order to press demands against individual employers. But true worker solidarity would overcome this emphasis on individual labor sectors and employers. Genuine efforts at solidarity would attempt to bridge sectoral, regional, and ideological differences to link all workers together in a common effort to understand and change the society-wide socioeconomic and political structures that permit employers to dominate and exploit them.

In contrast, the tactics spawned by a business-unionism approach to labor organizing are designed to meet immediate, concrete objectives within the general outlines of the distribution of power and other resources of a capitalist society. The tactics consequently focus on collective bargaining and negotiations in the interests of maintaining labor-business harmony. Strikes and other militant actions are considered only as last-ditch options, as are alliances with social sectors outside the labor community.[11]

An important caveat to this tactical pattern must be mentioned. In countries with governments opposed by Washington and the AFL-CIO, the labor federation encourages highly militant political and economic actions by its allies. Under most circumstances, however, those actions are mounted against *governments,* not management per se. Provocative activities such as strikes, general strikes, political demonstrations, and occupations of public buildings have been undertaken by foreign unions linked to the AFL-CIO in Chile, Nicaragua, Eastern Europe, and China during the past few years. On the other hand, in countries like El Salvador that are considered "friends of the U.S. government," the federation's allies usually steer clear of anti-government coalitions and demonstrations. This pattern only breaks down when the foreign unions find they cannot satisfy important needs as long as they stick with the moderate stands pushed by the U.S. federation.[12]

As alternatives to class-based analyses, the AFL-CIO and its institutes offer prescriptions for "apolitical" trade unionism aimed at increasing the size of the pie through enhanced productivity and labor's piece of the pie through collective bargaining. The notion of class struggle is inconsistent with the cooperative labor-business relations advocated by the AFL-CIO. This promotion of a so-called apolitical trade unionism, however, is a political choice with political outcomes. Refusing to question the underlying assumptions and relationships of capitalism, the U.S. federation has demonized radical responses to capitalist exploitation and failed to come to grips with the fact that "misery breeds militancy."[13] In so doing, the AFL-CIO has, intentionally or not, supported the global economic and political status quo.

The federation has given U.S. labor's official stamp of approval to political and economic systems that reflect U.S.-style concepts of free-market capitalism and minimal political participation. In the process, it has undermined movements for workplace control and democracy and rejected attempts to analyze and restructure fundamental relationships among owners, workers, and governments. When, as in Brazil (1964), the Dominican Republic (1965), and Chile (1973), it has found that radical movements were too strong, it has rejected even minimal electoral democracy and supported military coups. It has placed itself on the side of governments and elites that prop up the global dominance of the United States and the economic dominance of owners over workers.

From the Old to the New World Order

By enlisting foreign labor in a procapitalist pact generally supportive of U.S. business, the AFL-CIO added momentum to the expansion of U.S. transnational corporations abroad.[14] Labor's role in this endeavor has deep historical roots. Organized labor, business, and the governing elite in the United States have traditionally seen the third world as a source of raw materials useful in U.S. enterprises and as a market for goods produced by U.S. workers. Overseas investments were also considered necessary to absorb the excess capital produced by businesses in the United States.

As Alabama's Senator John T. Morgan warned in 1882, "Our home market is not equal to the demands of our producing and manufacturing classes and to the capital which is seeking employment...We must either enlarge the field of our traffic, or stop the business of manufacturing just where it is."[15] Somewhat later, during the depression of the 1890s, Secretary of State Walter Gresham worried that U.S. enterprises could "not afford constant employment for our labor." He proposed that the government act immediately "to enable our people to compete in foreign markets with Great Britain."[16]

For many years, U.S. expansion of corporate and political influence benefited U.S. unionists. Foreign investments generated profits that returned to the United States, were invested anew in domestic enterprises, and helped maintain salaries and other benefits. Raw materials obtained from abroad and overseas markets dominated by the United States were the ingredients of a thriving U.S. manufacturing sector. Higher wages and benefits, enhanced job security, and participation in the generalized wealth in the United States flowed to skilled workers from the profits of U.S. businesses with access to foreign markets and natural resources. From this perspective, acting as the entering wedge for U.S. business and helping to create procapitalist, pro-U.S. unions overseas once made sense in narrow material, if not moral, terms.

As a result of perspectives and payoffs like these, the AFL-CIO has tended to overlook or minimize worker exploitation that results from capitalist economic and political structures. Shortly after the 1964 military coup in Brazil—backed by the CIA and supported by Brazilian unions trained by the American Institute for Free Labor Development (AIFLD)—the AFL-CIO encouraged Brazilian workers to accept a wage freeze. The federation took this stance despite the brutality of the government, the reactionary intransigence of business, and runaway inflation. In a radio interview, William Doherty, then AIFLD's social projects director and its current executive director, explained, "You can't have the poor suffer more than the rich or the poor less than the rich, and if these proper checks and balances are built into the system, the Brazilian labor movement will cooperate in any type of wage freeze that may have to be employed to bring about stability."[17]

Doherty's comments were not just the product of the "anticommunism at all costs" delirium that swept the United States in the 1950s and early 1960s. They reflect an ideological perspective that continues to guide the AFL-CIO's foreign policy. In Poland, where the Solidarity trade union fired the imaginations of people around the world with its political and economic militancy, the Free Trade Union Institute (FTUI) is now promoting its brand of moderate, bread-and-butter unionism. Throughout the 1980s, the institute funneled major grants to Solidarity and its supporters for programs ranging from medical care to printing and distributing underground publications. Its interest was not in creating a powerful, pro-worker labor union, however, but in dumping the communist regime, a fact that became clear with the fall of the Jaruzelski government. With the rise to political power of

Solidarity, labor leaders from the U.S. institute found themselves close to the new government and to Solidarity-linked Polish organizations that advocated radical free-market economic policies. The U.S. federation pushed the Solidarity government's conservative economic strategies despite the harsh repercussions on Poland's workforce. A 1989 U.S. delegation to Poland, which included AFL-CIO President Lane Kirkland as well as business and government representatives, suggested that planned wage cuts would be difficult for the population but would provide an "important source of international competitive advantage" on the world market.[18]

A major goal of post-communist programs in Poland was to control potential worker unrest in response to economic restructuring. The U.S. delegation observed that unemployment could become "critical" and that "major worker unrest" during the transition to capitalism "could hamper Polish government efforts to make difficult long-term reforms that are needed." Both the delegation and various U.S. government-funded programs recommended calming this restive working population by providing short-term material aid funneled through private organizations such as labor unions. The delegation's report described this aid as a "social shield" designed to deflect some of the traumatic economic effects of the Polish restructuring.[19]

But in the new global economy, dampening labor militancy in one corner of the world has sharply negative consequences for workers in other countries, and the AFL-CIO's actions in Poland will likely prove short-sighted for both Polish and U.S. workers. Such has been the case in other regions where the U.S. federation has failed to encourage worker militancy. This fact is painfully clear along the U.S.-Mexico border, for example, where many U.S. workers have seen their jobs shipped south as employers chase the higher profits associated with Mexico's low wages and lax environmental standards.

One such case occurred at a Pillsbury-Green Giant plant in Watsonville, California. In January 1991, the company announced the layoff of several hundred Watsonville employees, while simultaneously expanding vegetable production at the company's plant in Irapuato, Mexico.[20] The relocation was carried out even though Pillsbury-Green Giant and its British parent company, Grand Metropolitan, hauled in pre-tax profits of $1.7 billion in 1990. Apparently these profits were not considered high enough to keep production in California, with its higher wages and stricter labor and environmental standards. Having spent an average of 14 years with the company, the Watsonville employees earned about $7.61 per hour with medical and retirement benefits under a union contract. In Irapuato, though, the company pays about $4 per day, with few benefits, thus increasing annual profits by

$6 million on wage savings alone. A 15-year Green Giant worker who was laid off in Watsonville spoke bitterly of the company's move: "We helped them make their millions, now we are left with nothing but backaches and twisted fingers."[21] In Irapuato, Green Giant workers cannot afford to feed their families on the pay they receive for their labor, and employees have been fired for attempting to organize a union.

According to Watsonville activist Mike Kostyal, the AFL-CIO itself has contributed to the problems being faced by workers in the United States and in other countries. Kostyal is the coordinator of the "Boycott Pillsbury-Green Giant" campaign of *Trabajadores Desplazados* (Displaced Workers), a group of laid-off Green Giant employees who have decided to fight back. The AFL-CIO, Kostyal observes, has been "woefully moribund" when it comes to organizing against business on an international level. By not fully communicating to its members the harsh conditions faced by labor overseas, and by failing to help foreign workers organize vigorous, unified unions, Kostyal explains, the U.S. federation has been unable to stem the loss of jobs for U.S. workers.[22]

The Watsonville example points out a glitch in the AFL-CIO's general support for global capitalism and the expansion of U.S. capital in particular: The material interests of U.S. labor are no longer being served by this expansion. On the contrary, U.S. workers are suffering from its effects, just as their foreign counterparts have been hurt in the past.

While western transnational corporations (TNCs) have prospered, both U.S. and foreign workers have suffered as capital has become less tied to a given country and more transnational in nature. In search of maximum profits, TNCs hop country to country, hoping to lower their wage bill while keeping productivity high. Cash-starved third world governments support this effort. The need for hard currency and jobs has prompted poor governments to compete globally for foreign investment by holding down wage rates and repressing labor.[23] A. Sivanandan, the director of London's Institute of Race Relations, eloquently described this process and the damage it does to workers overseas:

> The governments of the [underdeveloped countries], desperate not for development as such but the end to the unemployment that threatens their regimes, enter into a Dutch auction with each other, offering the multinational corporations cheaper and cheaper labour, de-unionized labour, captive labour, female labour and child labour—by removing whatever labour laws, whatever trade union

rights have been gained in the past from at least that part of the country, the [export-processing zone], which foreign capital chooses for its own.[24]

In the global economy, tragedies such as these do not stay neatly tucked away in distant, destitute, and isolated pockets of the third world. As the Watsonville experience demonstrates, what happens to workers in the underdeveloped world boomerangs back to hurt workers in industrialized countries as well. Runaway shops spur job insecurity, downward pressure on wage levels, and assaults on worker rights in developed countries like the United States. As the economy becomes more global, the trend has been toward the equalization of conditions for labor in both developed and underdeveloped countries, but that trend has been downward—toward the levels characteristic in the third world. And the AFL-CIO's traditional support for the U.S. government's foreign policy has only aggravated that trend. Whereas building militant, united, global labor movements is needed to reverse this course of events, the AFL-CIO's overseas programs—as in Poland—have often encouraged workers to abandon militancy and shun radicals in pursuit of narrow, sectoral goals.

Labor and Business: Hand in Hand

In its overseas activities, the AFL-CIO has been an ally in the expansion of U.S. business around the world and in the consequent exploitation of foreign workers. In some cases, it has actively joined with business in the pursuit of foreign economic and political objectives. In other cases, U.S. corporations have benefited as a by-product of the type of unionism promoted by the labor federation. As AIFLD official William Doherty told Congress, "Our collaboration [with business] takes the form of trying to make the investment climate more attractive and more inviting."[25] Peter Grace, head of the W.R. Grace conglomerate and then-chairman of AIFLD's board of trustees, explained bluntly that the institute "teaches workers to increase their company's business."[26]

Such attitudes have a long history. Organized labor's cooperative relationship with big business in the United States dates back to the turn of the century, but the postwar version of that collaboration was formalized by Nelson Rockefeller, head of the State Department's Office of Inter-American Affairs during World War II.[27] He encouraged a wartime coalition of labor, business, and the government that carried over into the Cold War era. Over the years, that cooperative relationship has been manifested in various forms. The American Federation of Labor's anticommunist activities in postwar Europe were financed by U.S. businesses, for example. Currently, both labor and business serve on the board of the U.S. government-funded National Endowment for Democracy (NED). A grant-making agency that finances pro-U.S. private groups overseas, NED supports politically active organizations in such strategic sectors as labor, business, and the media.

The American Institute for Free Labor Development provides perhaps the clearest example of the AFL-CIO's alliance with the business sector. From its inception until 1981, AIFLD's board of trustees included officials from big business as well as labor leaders and select Latin American bureaucrats. Major corporations with interests in Latin America—including Kennecott and Anaconda copper companies, ITT, Pan American World Airways, the Rockefellers, and W.R. Grace—were represented on the institute's board. These and some 90 other corporations with holdings in Latin America also supported AIFLD financially, although never in sums approaching U.S. government contributions.[28]

That J. Peter Grace held such a high position in AIFLD makes a travesty of the institute's claim to represent Latin American workers. A U.S. reporter described worker housing conditions on two of the tycoon's largest plantations as "distressingly dirty and crowded. Much of the housing is small, multiple, unpainted, and without running water. The streets alternate between mud and dust and contain debris and the leavings of freely running animals."[29] In 1960, when 3000 Peruvian workers struck a Grace facility, the company called in the police, who killed three workers and injured another sixteen.[30] AIFLD's other corporate backers were equally guilty of ill-treating their Latin American workers. ITT even helped bring down the democratically elected government of Salvador Allende in Chile, paving the way for the savage anti-union dictatorship that gripped the country for the next 16 years.

In 1981, following years of criticism regarding corporate involvement on the board, AIFLD restricted positions on its governing body to members of the labor community. But Grace promised that the business community would "continue to perform in a friendly and supportive capacity."[31]

None of this is meant to imply that the AFL-CIO is always a stooge for big business or that all businesses benefit directly from AFL-CIO operations. The federation's organizing efforts, material aid, trainings, and union-building activities do help many of its favored unions fight economistic battles against particular employers. As various analysts have shown, labor organizations in the third world desperately need material assistance such as copying equipment and vehicles in order to support their activities.[32] In addition, they benefit from educational services, given the complex economic and political factors they must take into account during negotiations and organizing campaigns. And the AFL-CIO's international support can be crucial during periods of government-sponsored repression. In the 1980s, for instance, the labor federation's Latin American arm publicized the cases of unionists under fire from Chile's dictatorial regime, and the AFL-CIO's pressure was an important factor in the U.S. government's belated decision to suspend Chile's tariff privileges in 1987.[33]

The problem is in the overall type of unionism supported by the federation overseas. The AFL-CIO and its regional institutes adhere to an anticommunist, pro-U.S., and procapitalist agenda that shapes their choice of beneficiaries. Unfortunately, this agenda often pits the labor institutes against nationalist and popular movements that are struggling to redistribute economic and political resources in a more equitable fashion. Even in the Chilean case, the AFL-CIO's supportive efforts focused on its allies in the United Workers Central, while failing to publicize the repression of more radical unionists. Tragically, the federation has acted similarly in El Salvador, where popular labor forces that oppose the rightist government and the skewed social system it protects have suffered merciless repression.

Despite positive rhetoric about backing worldwide worker rights and vigorous unions, the federation and its institutes have sabotaged worker unity, promoted conservative and apolitical trade unions, and built parallel unions to sap the strength of more broad-based and progressive labor organizations. In various cases—as with the Federation of Korean Trade Unions, the Brazilian General Confederation of Labor, and the Haitian Federation of Trade Union Workers under Jean-Claude Duvalier—this has meant that the U.S. federation has sided with unions that have been controlled or influenced by rightwing governments. Each of these factors has undermined the vitality of foreign labor movements. They have stimulated infighting and impeded the formation of coalitions that are needed to press worker demands against employers and governments.

Bipartisan Consensus

Rather than just being another player, the AFL-CIO has assumed a uniquely important role in U.S. expansionism. This expansionism is fueled by a bipartisan agreement that it is acceptable for the United States to intervene in the affairs of other countries. Described euphemistically by one study as a "sober sense of mission about [U.S.] responsibilities to struggling democracies elsewhere," this consensus has characterized most of U.S. foreign policy since the late 1800s.[34]

Even prior to that time, doctrines such as Manifest Destiny and the Monroe Doctrine undergirded U.S. expansion of both its territory and its sphere of influence. Democrats and Republicans, big labor, and businesses that could profit by U.S. internationalism tended to back such expansion. A given sector might oppose a particular intervention—the AFL opposed the outright annexation of Hawaii, for instance—but, in general, organized labor fell in behind U.S. adventures abroad.[35]

Throughout the twentieth century, the United States played an ever-larger role on the world stage, but the collapse of the European powers after World War II opened the globe to a vastly expanded U.S. presence. The United States soon came to dominate the international economy. In 1950, the United States produced a full 40 percent of the world's goods and services. At the same time, Washington built up its war machine. Under Truman, military spending jumped from $13 billion in 1950 to $50 billion in 1953, with only a small percentage earmarked for the Korean conflict. With the leverage provided by its economic and military resources, the United States restructured the international economy in its favor.[36] It forced trade barriers down in Europe and began pushing into new markets in Asia and Africa, protected by newly established military bases around the world.

During the activist years from 1945 until the mid-1960s, bipartisan acceptance of U.S. expansionism supported a number of initiatives that extended the global reach of the United States. These included the Marshall Plan, the North Atlantic Treaty Organization (NATO), the Southeast Asia Treaty Organization, the Alliance for Progress, and the Vietnam conflict. Massive public opposition to the Vietnam War rattled the foundations of this consensus, but efforts both in and out of government were soon launched to reinvigorate national willingness to extend U.S. power overseas.[37]

By the early 1980s, that consensus had recuperated considerably. Over the next few years, backed by substantial public support, the United States invaded Grenada and Panama; bombed Libya; sent U.S. military "advisers" to El Salvador; backed anticommunist guerrilla movements in Nicaragua, Angola, Afghanistan, and Southeast Asia; mined Nicaraguan harbors; and launched a full-scale war in the Persian Gulf. Washington also intervened in electoral activities in various countries, including Nicaragua, Eastern Europe, and the Philippines. Moreover, by 1991, Washington-funded advisers and technical teams were swarming through Eastern Europe, helping to restructure political and economic systems following the collapse of the previous governments.

Acting in tandem with official initiatives, the AFL-CIO boosts overseas unions that oppose worker movements holding radical positions. This holds true even when the interests of labor would be better served by more radical unions. In the Philippines, for example, the Asian institute of the AFL-CIO has fought a pitched battle for the hearts and minds of Filipino workers and peasants through its longtime affiliate, the Trade Union Congress of the Philippines (TUCP). Established in 1975 when the country was under martial law, the TUCP was the only legally recognized union federation under the dictatorship of Ferdinand Marcos. The labor congress maintained friendly relations with the Marcos government and a docile attitude toward business. Until 1984, Marcos was the featured speaker at the TUCP's annual May Day Breakfast.[38] The trade union congress served on tripartite commissions with government and business representatives, setting wages and working conditions, and helping establish the conditions for loans from the International Monetary Fund.[39]

The TUCP has had ties to rightwing organizations in the country as well as to government and business. For instance, a national meeting of vigilante groups was held at union headquarters in March 1987.[40] Likewise, the first two Philippine conferences of the Confederation of the Associations for the Unification of the Societies of the Americas (CAUSA), the political arm of the Reverend Sun Myung Moon's Unification Church, were held at the union federation's headquarters. At one of those conferences, Celia Laurel—head of CAUSA in the Philippines and wife of the country's ultra-conservative vice president under President Corazón Aquino—presented a paper stating the continued need for U.S. military bases in the Philippines.[41]

As far as business is concerned, the Philippine trade union congress has called for deregulation of the business and labor sectors in order to "promote the spirit of free initiative."[42] Some TUCP-affiliated unions have been notoriously submissive to employers. In one case, on the island of Cebu, an affiliated union negotiated a five cent per day increase in wages each year for collective bargaining agreements that spanned nine years. Each year, however, the union allowed the company not to pay the increase, arguing that it unfairly burdened the company.[43]

The TUCP's major labor opponent is the militant *Kilusang Mayo Uno* (KMU). The largest labor organization in the Philippines, the KMU calls for a democratic socialist economic system, national control over the country's natural resources, and the removal of U.S. military bases. The KMU has also advocated a more comprehensive agrarian reform than the TUCP and has generally pushed for more favorable employer concessions to workers. In objective terms, it would seem that the

KMU's policy stands better serve the interests of labor. But the U.S. federation's support for the trade union congress helps broaden the base of the Aquino government and keeps at least certain sectors of the working classes in a procapitalist coalition favorable to the U.S. presence in the country.

In the United States as well, the positions taken by the AFL-CIO through convention resolutions, congressional testimony, publications, and public appearances help to maintain the participation of U.S. labor in this bipartisan consensus. "Action Bulletins" published by AIFLD, for example, promote allied groups such as the Salvadoran National Union of Workers and Campesinos (UNOC), while recommending strict guidelines for U.S. labor activism.

In one such case, a March 19, 1989 bulletin called for U.S. unionists to write letters to Salvadoran government, political, and guerrilla leaders protesting the violence of the Left and the Right. The American labor institute and its Salvadoran ally drew parallels between the violence of the guerrillas and that of the rightwing. They criticized human rights violations by government security forces. The bulletin also included a sentence calling on the United States to halt military aid to the Salvadoran government until the military was purged of human rights violators. But in making the left and right wings in El Salvador seem equivalent, the bulletin drew a partial picture of the truth and boosted the fortunes of a brutal government friendly to Washington and U.S. business. The bulletin ignored the well-documented ties among the Salvadoran security forces, government institutions, and the right wing. It overlooked the umbilical dependence of those same institutions upon U.S. government funding, technical assistance, training, and diplomatic support. It failed to expose the Salvadoran conflict as a class war between overexploited working and peasant classes and entrenched elites, and, as such, a logical outgrowth of an economic system whose major features Washington and its Salvadoran allies would preserve.

Instead, the bulletin decried the violence of "extremists," sidestepping entirely the underlying motivations of the conflict in general and leftwing violence in particular. Furthermore, despite the throwaway sentence about cutting off U.S. military aid, the publication did not recommend putting pressure on U.S. political leaders to demand this action. Nor did it recommend other actions, such as the suspension or withdrawal of Salvadoran tariff privileges that allowed free entry of many of the country's exports into the United States. By framing the issues in these terms and by narrowing the recommended actions to those taken against Salvadoran political leaders, AIFLD implicitly contributed to Washington's policy of support for the repressive—

though capitalist and anticommunist—government in El Salvador. At the same time, it shaped a deceptive explanation of that policy and the Salvadoran conflict which it transmitted to its members.

Anticommunism and the AFL-CIO

The labor federation's distorted explanations of world events such as those described above regarding El Salvador spring largely from the organization's anticommunist worldview. As one close friend of the AFL-CIO has said, "The central preoccupation of American labor in the field of foreign affairs...has been to mobilize democratic forces to counter the threat posed by totalitarianism."[44] But the AFL-CIO defined "democratic" and "totalitarian" labor movements in East/West terms, perceiving even democratically organized leftwing and non-aligned union movements as dangerous allies of the Soviet Union. In his much-cited essay on U.S. labor's foreign policy, pro-labor activist Carl Gershman observed that the AFL-CIO considered itself locked in a mortal struggle with the Soviet Union for the allegiance of the world's workers.[45] Communism, George Meany once declared, is an "ultra-reactionary movement...making the free trade unions its first and foremost target."[46]

The officials behind the making of the AFL-CIO's foreign policy, men like Jay Lovestone and Irving Brown, were cold warriors before official U.S. policy turned in that direction under President Harry Truman in 1947.[47] A founding member of the U.S. Communist Party and former head of the party in the United States, Lovestone later turned aggressively anticommunist. Described by a journalist as "part cloak and dagger, part cloak and suit," Lovestone directed the AFL's Free Trade Union Committee, set up in Europe during World War II to help anticommunist labor organizations fight both the Axis powers and communist worker movements. After the war, Lovestone became a major force behind the construction of the AFL's anticommunist foreign policy.[48] He later headed the AFL's powerful department of international affairs. In both positions, he recruited like-minded activists like Irving Brown as field organizers or to staff important policy-making positions. Brown, a chief foreign policy lieutenant of the AFL-CIO who would eventually become its director of international affairs, served for 40 years as a link between the AFL-CIO and U.S. intelligence services in Africa, Asia, and Europe. In describing Brown's ubiquitous presence, a union associate said, "Irving was everywhere, but he...had a negative approach. All he wanted to do was to short circuit the communists."[49]

The federation's top officials have remained more hawkish than Washington even under big-stick administrations such as those of

Lyndon Johnson and Richard Nixon. Likewise, the federation maintained an easy overseas partnership with the rigidly anticommunist government of Ronald Reagan during the 1980s. In contrast, as in postwar Africa or Spain under Franco, the federation often pursued policies that were anti-colonial and anti-fascist even when, in the words of Sidney Lens, the U.S. government was "willing to sleep in the same bed with these forces."[50] But, as in Vietnam, the federation's opposition to colonialism and fascism was always subordinate to its anticommunism.

Under these men, the AFL-CIO became committed to fighting communism with whatever means necessary, ranging from the building of pro-U.S. labor movements to the backing of U.S. militarism. Those who developed the federation's foreign policy considered the conflict with communism a "permanent war," according to one analyst, in which "only one side [could] survive and the other be destroyed. Consequently, as in hot war, you do not speak of the good points of the enemy or your own bad points, and you permit no charity to neutrals."[51]

Attitudes such as these led to a siege mentality and tunnel vision regarding radical movements in the third world. The AFL-CIO's anticommunism blended a fear of Soviet expansion, genuinely felt by many in the postwar years, with a fear of all forms of radicalism. The federation became not only anticommunist, said one union activist, but "anti-left. It even opposed the democratic left." As this activist explained, the leadership of the AFL-CIO held "idiosyncratic, fundamentalist views" of communism and leftwing movements for social change. "The anticommunism of the federation is excessively broad, it's not just anti-Stalinist, but is anti-leftist, anti-democratic left," this top union staffer observed. "Even the State Department is more receptive to the democratic left than these guys [in the federation hierarchy], especially when you appeal to them on the basis of pluralist values."[52]

And in the postwar period, such attitudes were crucially misguided. In response to outrageous inequities, worker and social movements that demanded fundamental, even revolutionary change, sprang up throughout the developing world, especially after the success of the Cuban Revolution. Assuming that these movements were inspired or manipulated by the Soviet Union, the AFL-CIO climbed into a "Cold War straitjacket."[53]

The federation developed a policy of "shunning" unions that were considered part of the communist camp. It implemented its anticommunism by redbaiting outspoken radical unionists and attempting to outlaw the political participation of communists in unions. Like other anticommunists, the federation helped to maintain order and an often-repressive status quo because upheaval and dissent were thought to open the door for communist infiltration, masterminded from Moscow. In the Cold War battle, the AFL-CIO found itself on the side of conservative anti-union forces like board member J. Peter Grace, who put the alliance in these terms:

> The choice in Latin America is between democracy and communism. We...cannot allow communist propaganda to divide us between liberal and conservatives, as between business and labor, or between the American people and their government. Above all, we have to act together as Americans defending our interests abroad. The [American Institute for Free Labor Development] is an outstanding example of a national consensus effectively at work for the best interests of the people of Latin America.[54]

But in misreading the nature and objectives of militant social and nationalist conflict in East/West, communist/"democratic" terms, the U.S. labor federation placed itself on the wrong side of the fight for justice and equity. In the words of two labor activists, it violated "the fundamental principle of solidarity" by purging communists from its own ranks and forcing them to be excluded from other union movements.[55] Because the Left was often the source of much of the dynamism and vision of these militant nationalist movements, the U.S. federation sapped the energy of progressive forces and participated in the "barren defense of the status quo" characteristic of much of U.S. foreign policy during the postwar years.[56] It also marginalized itself from the world's progressive labor movements. As labor's friend Carl Gershman indicated, "The AFL-CIO's firmness of conviction...is...responsible for American labor's relative isolation on the world scene."[57]

Overseas Adventures

The character of the relationship between the U.S. government and the AFL-CIO has varied in response to political and economic changes in both the domestic and international arenas. During wartime and in regions where the United States has carried out military operations or counterinsurgency actions—in World War II, postwar Europe, Vietnam, Central America, and the Philippines, for example—organized labor has acted as a full-fledged government operative. At other times and in areas less strategically important to the United States, the AFL-CIO's relationship with Washington has been more independent. Similarly, in times of exceptional economic pressure on labor, there are more discrepancies between labor's policy positions and those of Washington. The decade of the 1980s was one such period, when the decline of U.S. competitiveness in the global economy coupled with the anti-union philosophies of U.S. administrations drove a wedge between the AFL-CIO and Washington on certain foreign policy issues.

Disagreements between the U.S. government and the AFL-CIO have arisen particularly in the realm of domestic policy and have been accentuated during times of government suppression of U.S. union activities. During the 1980s, for example, the AFL-CIO consistently, although ineffectively, resisted the Reagan administration's union-busting efforts. It also opposed privatization of U.S. government assets such as Conrail and supported tax overhauls that protected middle and low income earners while increasing taxes on the wealthy. The federation participated in the "Housing Now" march on Washington in October 1989, backed legislation requiring that workers be notified of potential work-related medical hazards, and endorsed Democratic presidential candidates in the national elections.

On foreign policy issues too, despite an overall congruence between organized labor's stands and those of the U.S. government, not all of the AFL-CIO's positions line up with Washington's.[58] On certain economic issues which impact on U.S. labor—such as free trade agreements and free trade zones—the AFL-CIO counters current government policies by backing protectionist legislation designed to safeguard U.S. jobs and income levels.[59] Such stands do not hold across the board, however. In El Salvador, for example, where AIFLD has been a stalwart player in Washington's counterinsurgency project, the AFL-CIO's opposition to U.S.-pushed free trade zones has been muted.

For the most part, though, the AFL-CIO has been a tireless ally of Washington on national security issues and a ready partner in the U.S. government's overseas adventurism. This book attempts to disclose the nature of this partnership and the characteristics of the labor federation's activities abroad. For the first time, it makes an effort to look at those activities in all regions simultaneously and to disclose as much as possible of the federation's decision-making structure and the sources and effects of its foreign policy.

The book sketches the major features of the role played by the AFL-CIO in the overseas expansion of the United States. Chapter One explores the relationship of the AFL-CIO to the U.S. government. Historical trends are highlighted, but more significantly, this section discloses the labor federation's dependence on government funding and logistical assistance. The decision-making structure and process of the AFL-CIO regarding foreign policy issues are also examined. Chapter Two explores the relationship of U.S. organized labor to the larger network of private organizations involved in the current wave of Washington-funded "democracy-building" worldwide.

Chapter Three sketches out the structural characteristics of the labor federation's international apparatus. It explores the history, objectives, and arenas of operation of the international institutes and the connections of the labor federation to international labor bodies. Chapter Four summarizes the foreign operations of the labor institutes, including the types of projects conducted, their effects on foreign labor, and their payoffs for U.S. expansionism.

Chapter Five concludes the book with an overview of the contradictory influences at work on the AFL-CIO's foreign policy. It looks at current trends in the global economy that are shaping the international labor environment and makes predictions about the federation's future relationship to and effects on overseas labor movements. It also suggests the broad outlines of an alternative foreign policy for labor, one that has been in the process of construction over the last decade by elements of progressive labor and the rank and file.

CHAPTER ONE
Joining Hands with Washington

Publicly, the AFL-CIO and its institutes stress their independence from government. A closer look, however, tells a different story. The current partnership between the AFL-CIO and the U.S. government has historical roots dating to the early part of this century. Now, dependent on Washington for funding and logistical assistance, the institutes often function as vital appendages for the government in international labor affairs. Without these government resources, the institutes would be unable to carry out their projects overseas. Without the AFL-CIO's help, the U.S. government would be hard-pressed to build a base of support among foreign workers.

Despite the importance of these ties, the foreign activities of the federation are cloaked in secrecy, making democratic accountability nearly impossible to achieve. Washington's monitoring of its government-funded labor programs is imprecise, infrequent, and perfunctory—at least in the public record. The State Department, in fact, has a closer relationship with the institutes than does their main funding source, the Agency for International Development. In addition, the federation's decision-making about foreign policies and programs takes place behind a nearly impenetrable screen. Backroom planning by labor elites determines the federation's activities abroad and the relation of those activities to U.S. foreign policy. The result is a network of labor operations intertwined with the foreign policy apparatus of the U.S. government but insufficiently called to account for its activities and their consequences.

Foreign Policy Tool

The international institutes of the AFL-CIO are favorites of the U.S. Congress. The special importance their labor projects hold for Congress is reflected in the legislation that authorizes funding for the AFL-CIO's overseas programs. The institute's foreign operations receive funds from the Agency for International Development (AID) under provisions of the Foreign Assistance Act of 1961. That act declares it U.S. policy to help people in developing countries "to build the economic, political, and social institutions which will improve the quality of their lives." It also includes a specific mandate "to strengthen free labor unions." Moreover, it promotes various methods for supporting international development, such as working through the "private sector," including "free labor unions," to the "maximum extent possible." Similarly, the Department of Labor and the AFL-CIO have a "consultative relationship" that is written into congressional legislation dealing with trade and labor issues.[1]

Labor's funding from the National Endowment for Democracy (NED) also illustrates congressional favor for the labor institutes. Authorization for NED's funding is contained in yearly foreign affairs authorization acts. In these authorization acts, a major portion of the endowment's funding each year has been earmarked for the Free Trade Union Institute, to be funneled through FTUI and the other labor institutes. Although funds are also earmarked for the Center for International Private Enterprise, another core grantee of the endowment, the labor institute has always been awarded the lion's share.

Indeed, the international institutes of the AFL-CIO get the overwhelming majority of their funding from the U.S. government, a fact which belies their claim to be private organizations independent of Washington. The funds are channeled through the U.S. Information Agency (USIA) and AID, an arm of the State Department. In 1987, for example, direct grants from AID, together with USIA grants which were passed through the National Endowment for Democracy, accounted for 98 percent of the institutes' funding, while the labor federation itself contributed a mere 2 percent toward its foreign activities.[2]

These figures are consistent with prior funding patterns. The American Institute for Free Labor Development, for example, received 89 percent of its financing from AID between 1962 and 1967. The AFL-CIO's contribution during those years tallied only 6 percent, while corporate funding provided 5 percent of the total. By 1971 the Latin American institute was the fifteenth largest recipient of AID contracts, and by 1981, AID provided some 95 percent of the institute's budget.[3] As stated in an AID-contracted evaluation of AIFLD grant programs in 1986, "AID has been virtually the exclusive supporter of AIFLD for 20 years, and is likely to continue supporting the organization into the indefinite future."[4]

Although most private organizations that receive government funding are required to raise at least 20 percent of their funds from nongovernment sources, the AFL-CIO's institutes are exempted from this provision because they are considered "intermediaries in conducting AID's program."[5] In fact, AID's Office of Private and Voluntary Cooperation does not even have a funding relationship with the labor institutes.[6] Instead—reflecting the centrality of the labor projects to government policies—it is AID's front-line departments, its regional bureaus, country missions, and special projects offices, that act as the conduits for labor funds.

Richard Whitaker, the Democracy Program Officer in AID's Bureau for Asia and Private Enterprise, observed that the exemption from the private fundraising requirement works against the independence of the institutes.[7] "[The Asian-American Free Labor Institute] doesn't have to meet the privateness test," Whitaker explained, "and is therefore dependent on the U.S. government. To be reliant that much on the U.S. government should be an issue for them [AAFLI]." The privateness test is important, he said, "because otherwise you have essentially a government program."

Funds from AID flow into the institutes from various sources. Regional core grants provide the most consistent and largest amount of funding to each of the institutes. They are channeled through the agency's regional bureaus for Africa, Latin America and the Caribbean (LAC), Asia/Private Enterprise, and the Near East/Europe. Other funds may be awarded to the institutes for union-to-union programs carried out by individual unions through their international trade secretariats. Still other AID funds flow to the institutes through special project offices at the agency. In 1990, for instance, the Democracy Initiatives and Human Rights Program provided funding to the Free Trade Union Institute, as well as to the labor institutes for Latin America and Asia.[8]

In other cases, AID country missions fund the institutes directly out of their own budgets. The grants, contracts, and cooperative agreements which are financed from the missions are monitored by the missions as well. In 1990, Latin American mission programs were funded in Bolivia, Costa Rica, El Salvador, Ecuador, Guatemala, Honduras, and Nicaragua.[9]

Funding from AID is channeled directly to the institutes, bypassing the international affairs department of the AFL-CIO. Under normal circumstances, the institute budgets specify where and how the money will be spent. AIFLD, for example, splits its regional core grant among its country offices, education department, agrarian union projects, the George Meany Center, and administration. Exceptions to this general pattern occur when AID missions or agency headquarters contract with the institutes for specific projects determined by AID itself.

In 1987, AID grants to the institutes reflected the following distribution:[10]

American Institute for Free Labor Development
General grant $9,237,000
Cooperatives (El Salvador) $2,500,000
Operational Program Grants
Costa Rica $322,940
Ecuador $139,855
Panama $148,350
Honduras $82,000
Guatemala $516,690
Other
Haiti $206,700
Grenada $176,800

African-American Labor Center
General grant $3,125,000
Sudan supplement $480,000
South Africa supplement $875,000

Asian-American Free Labor Institute
General grant $3,700,000
Philippines supplement $1,250,000

Free Trade Union Institute
No AID grants were funneled to FTUI in 1987.

In recent years, the general grants to the labor institutes have been supplemented by monies channeled through special offices at AID which focus on "human rights" and "democracy-building." In 1990, for example, the Asian institute was awarded $3 million for its core grant plus additional funding from the democracy program and human rights office, distributed as follows: $300,000, Thailand; 118,000, Indonesia; 25,000, Bangladesh; 30,000, Philippines; 40,000, Thailand[11]; 25,000, Tunisia.[12]

Likewise, FTUI was awarded $2.9 million from AID under the East European Democracy Program in 1990.[13] The projects funded by these grants were carried out in Bulgaria, Czechoslovakia, and Hungary.[14]

At times official U.S. funds are designated for specific projects with clear economic and political payoffs for U.S. business and the administration of the day. In 1985 more than $63,000 in government funds were funneled through the A. Philip Randolph Education Fund, an arm of the AFL-CIO, to sponsor a labor conference on South Africa. Major speakers at the event—who included representatives of corporations with holdings in the country—endorsed notions of limited sanctions compatible with the Reagan administration's policy of "constructive engagement."[15] Early in 1990, AID funds were specifically earmarked for institution-building, organizing drives, election-related activities, and media efforts of union groups in Poland, Hungary, Bulgaria, Czechoslovakia, and Romania.[16] The AID financing helped U.S. labor sweep into the vacuum of post-Cold War Eastern Europe with its probusiness philosophies and prescriptions for a compliant labor sector, much as CIA funding helped the AFL-CIO shape the European labor scene following World War II.

A hefty share of funding from the National Endowment for Democracy has always been funneled through the Free Trade Union Institute. This is not surprising given the strategic importance of the labor sector in NED's "democracy-building" strategy, as well as labor's congressional backing, the federation's friends on NED's board, and the institutional vigor and international presence of the AFL-CIO's regional institutes. During NED's first two operating years, FTUI

Table 1:
National Endowment for Democracy Funding to the
Free Trade Union Institute 1984-1989*

1984	$11.0 million
1985	$13.8 million
1986	$4.3 million
1987	$4.8 million
1988	$6.8 million**
1989	$6.1 million**
1990	$7.8 million**

Sources: Free Trade Union Institute, "Defending Freedom of Association: Private Work in the Public Interest: The AFL-CIO and the National Endowment for Democracy," 1987, report submitted to Congress with testimony of Eugenia Kemble in *Departments of Commerce, Justice, and State, the Judiciary, and Related Agencies Appropriations for 1989*, Hearings before a subcommittee of the Committee on Appropriations, House of Representatives, 100th Congress, Second Session, Part 5, March 28, 1988; Interview with Peter Kosciewicz, National Endowment for Democracy, October 31, 1990; and National Endowment for Democracy, Annual Report, 1990.

*For distribution to the other institutes as well as for grants administered by FTUI itself.
**The figures for 1988-1990 include AID funds channeled through the NED to FTUI and earmarked by Congress for particular country projects.

received a full 68 percent of the grant monies provided by the endowment.[17] By 1986, budgetary cutbacks at NED, as well as administrative changes in grant allocation policies at the endowment led to major reductions in grants to FTUI. By the late 1980s, however, FTUI's piece of the pie had begun to expand once again, supplemented by special AID funds passed through NED but earmarked for labor projects in places like the Philippines, Eastern Europe, and Central America. (See Table 1.)

In addition to this dependence on government funding, the institutes receive logistical assistance and feedback on programs from government agencies and U.S. embassies. In Kenya, for example, representatives from the U.S. embassy and the U.S. Information Agency helped AALC-sponsored labor educators from the University of Alabama develop materials for a local labor education program.[18] Moreover some institute projects are responses to particular government requests. Following the U.S. invasion of Grenada in October 1983, for instance, a report written by a U.S. government interagency team recommended that AIFLD should assume responsibility for restructuring and training the country's unions. Redirecting union radicalism and strengthening "democratic" labor leaders were the objectives of the program.[19]

In another example, the White House in June 1986 asked for AIFLD's assistance in Haiti "because of the presence of radical labor unions and the high risk that other unions may become radicalized."[20] But radicalization of the Haitian labor force seems a quite reasonable response to Haiti's dire poverty (the country is the poorest in the western hemisphere), stupendously skewed income distribution, and dismal working conditions. Even after the flight of longtime dictator Jean-Claude Duvalier in February 1986, workers were fired for seeking to organize, and their strikes and protests were met with violent repression by the armed forces and by groups of thugs hired by employers.[21] The main targets of these anti-labor activities have been workers associated with the Autonomous Central of Haitian Workers (CATH), an outspoken proponent of political reform as well as labor rights and the most militant of Haitian union groupings. CATH is not aligned with any international union confederation, and its neutrality in the Cold War and militance on the labor front have made it suspect in the eyes of the U.S. federation. Another major target of repression has been a CATH breakaway faction, the Autonomous Central of Haitian Workers-Confederation of Latin American Workers (CATH-CLAT), so named because of its affiliation with the association of Christian Democratic unions in Latin America known as the Confederation of Latin American Workers (CLAT).

In stark contrast to the treatment of these two more militant federations, the conservative Federation of Trade Union Workers (FOS) has largely been allowed to continue its organizing and institution-building activities. The American Institute for Free Labor Development helped to establish FOS in 1984 in order to qualify Haiti to participate in the Caribbean Basin Initiative (CBI). CBI is a U.S.-sponsored regional development program that permits qualified countries to export products to the United States without paying the usual duties, assuming they meet certain requirements such as allowing workers to join unions. FOS was the only recognized union grouping under Duvalier, a cosmetic formality that allowed Haiti—and U.S. assembly plants—duty free access to the U.S. market under CBI. FOS continues to be the major recipient of U.S. funding for labor in Haiti. Other associations, such as the Independent General Organization of Haitian Workers (OGITH), have also received U.S. government funding funneled through AIFLD for institution-building, organizing, media efforts, and election-related activities.

In addition to fielding requests from the U.S. government to work in specific countries, labor representatives participate in government-sponsored interagency meetings to strategize on policy and its implementation. In January 1990, for example, the AFL-CIO joined representatives from the National Endowment for Democracy, State Department, AID, and private organizations like AmeriCares and Project Hope to plan aid to Poland. In Africa, proposals for the African institute's one-shot "impact projects" are first submitted either to the U.S. ambassador or AID Mission Director in a given country in order to make sure that the activity is in agreement with U.S. government policy objectives.[22] Furthermore, the institutes' AID grant proposals and evaluations are written with reference to AID country objectives, with labor activities selected on the basis of their compatibility with agency goals.

The federation and its institutes have working relationships with other government agencies as well. For instance, they and their affiliated unions select candidates for U.S. government-funded programs focusing on labor. The Latin American institute recommends unionists for USIA's international visitor program, for example, and helps make arrangements for these visits in the United States. It also selects candidates for trainings which are coordinated through the Department of Labor.[23]

As discussed below, the labor institutes historically have provided a channel through which the CIA could penetrate foreign labor sectors. They have offered a useful cover for intelligence operatives and supported undercover operations. In fact, both midlevel field

staff and top level members of each of the institutes have been identified as intelligence agents who operated with the direct assistance of
U.S. embassies and the CIA overseas. Such channels continue to be
available today even if actual revelations of CIA labor operations and
disclosure of active operatives working under CIA cover have not been
forthcoming under the conservative U.S. governments of the 1980s.

Secrecy and Democratic Accountability

According to a publication of the Asian institute, government
funds to the AFL-CIO's foreign labor operations "are voted on openly
by Congress after public hearings, and get intense public scrutiny by
Congress, by the Government Accounting Office, by the press, and by
others, more so in fact than most other publicly funded programs."[24]
In fact, however, because of their legal status as private organizations,
the regional institutes of the AFL-CIO are spared intense scrutiny in
Congress and their activities for the most part are shielded from public
exposure and debate. A congressional staff member deeply involved
in labor issues commented bluntly: "There's not a more unaccountable
strain of foreign policy in the last 25 years than the international labor
movement [of the AFL-CIO]."[25]

According to procedure and legislation, government-funded
labor projects are overseen by the funding agency and by Congress.
However, the monitoring performed by these oversight bodies is too
lax to provide an adequate measure of institute activities or of their
impact on foreign unions and political events. AID, NED, and Congress
typically rely on the self-reporting of the institutes as the basis for their
appraisals of labor projects.[26] This author was told repeatedly that there
was better understanding of and interest in the AFL-CIO's foreign
operations in the State Department than in the funding and oversight
bodies controlled by the U.S. public's elected representatives. In
addition, the grant and contract agreements which describe the work
to be performed by the institutes are often written in such general terms
that it is difficult to determine the precise nature of the activity or to
measure its impact, making it nearly impossible to hold the federation
accountable for its activities. These criticisms reflect those made by
the Senate Foreign Relations Committee as far back as 1968, when a
staff report found that "[In its work with the American Institute for
Free Labor Development] AID has not been able to provide the specific
guidance or to maintain the surveillance normally associated with
sound technical service contract arrangements."[27]

In like fashion, superficial accounting and oversight procedures
at the National Endowment for Democracy impede disclosure of the
details of labor grants.[28] Much of the planning and review is oral—

without written record or with only a minimal written record devoid of identifying or evaluative details. Its labor grants are rarely subjected to performance evaluations conducted by independent contractors. Instead, the bulk of the grants are evaluated by the institutes themselves, through quarterly and end-of-the-year progress reports to the endowment.

Outside evaluations of AID-funded institute projects do occur, although they are infrequent and cursory. As an example, a 1986 evaluation of AIFLD's core grant programs was conducted by a private contractor at AID's request and with AID funding. The last formal outside evaluation of the institute's overall program had occurred in 1975.[29] The evaluation team found that AIFLD had effectively used its resources to "support free democratic labor movements" and, in general, reported positively on the institute's activities. But, in keeping with the terms of the agreement signed with AID, the team did not evaluate a variety of projects, including several programs that were contracted through AID country missions.

Jack Francis, chief of the strategy development division in AID's Latin America and Caribbean office, said planning and reporting on labor projects has been "hit or miss" and outcomes difficult to evaluate.[30] Traditionally, he said, the Latin American institute had provided semi-annual reports to AID which gave figures on the number of seminars held, the number of unionists trained, and similar data. But the outcome of such activities, Francis said, "was difficult to measure."

AID is now trying to get a better handle on the reporting process, according to both Francis and Richard Whitaker of AID's Asia and Private Enterprise bureau. The Latin American and Asian labor institutes will be required to make quarterly reports which include both financial and program data. In AIFLD's case, the institute's country program directors will be expected to make qualitative evaluations of the effects of labor projects.

However, AID itself will not be increasing its own field visits, which traditionally have been sporadic and limited in scope. Whitaker says that he and others at the Washington office have to rely on their country missions as their "eyes and ears in the field" for on-site estimations of the impact of the AFL-CIO's foreign operations.[31] Site visits are too expensive for AID to conduct regularly. Moreover, as described below, AID's field officers are ill-equipped to perform such evaluations and are generally uninterested in labor projects. Because of factors such as these, the labor institutes will essentially continue to mark their own report cards, and these self-appraisals will continue to form the basis of most of AID's evaluations.

Tracking the funding path through government documents which purport to describe AID funding for the institutes is an exercise in confusion. Documents describing technical service contracts and grants cover multiyear allocations and do not provide breakdowns for individual years. Moreover, the summaries of the projects for which grants or contracts were awarded are excessively general. In 1988, for example, AID's report on regional core grants and technical service contracts to the Asian institute covered a period of four fiscal years and totaled $7 million. The contract description read, "Grantee shall provide partial support for an AAFLI program directed toward strengthening free and democratic trade unions." Other descriptions can, however, be instructive. A contract for $140,000, covering fiscal years 1986 through 1988, provided AIFLD with funds to offer "protective services" to its Central American staff.

It is just as difficult to extract useful information about labor projects from AID's annual Congressional Presentation. The financial information offered in the Congressional Presentation is somewhat easier to decipher than that presented in the documents on technical service contracts and grants: Actual expenditures are compared to obligated funds for multiyear periods and are broken down by individual years. But because the major support comes in the form of regional core grants, data on labor grants is lumped under the regional program offerings, and actual activities in individual countries are generally not specified. Even in countries like El Salvador, where AID frequently funds labor projects directly through its country budget, there are few descriptions of the actual projects or their beneficiaries. Further complicating the nearly hopeless effort, funding from the country missions is not included in the Congressional Presentation and is not readily available—if at all—to AID personnel in Washington.

To get more detail, one must request copies of the institute's government and NED grant agreements, evaluations, and annual reports through provisions of the Freedom of Information Act. These documents are much more complete, although detail on any given country is usually sparing. Using such documents, it is possible in most cases to identify the names of unions supported and the general kinds of activities conducted, but the political significance of their activities is often impossible to determine. This is an especially important omission because of the overwhelming importance of political factors in institute programs. Even a 1980 government audit of AIFLD found that its operations tended to be "political in nature rather than for developmental purposes."[32]

Even with documents received under the Freedom of Information Act, there is another obstacle blocking those who wish to hold the labor institutes accountable for their activities overseas. The actual amount of funding provided in a particular country is not always included in these documents, nor are explicit dollar breakdowns or explanations given for such broad categories as "education and social programs," "consultants," and "participant training." Without such information, ranking the projects in terms of their priority and importance to the U.S. government and to the institutes is not possible. Nor is it possible to determine the significance or usefulness of these programs for the foreign beneficiaries.

Despite the large amount of funding from AID to the institutes, AID field officers are frequently unfamiliar with in-country labor programs. According to a 1986 evaluation of many of AIFLD's programs, the senior staff of AID's Latin America and Caribbean office in Washington was familiar with, interested in, and concerned about AIFLD's programs. In the field, however, the evaluating team found there to be "considerably less interest and hence inadequate communication" between AID and AIFLD.[33]

According to a program officer at AID responsible for overseeing Asian labor projects, the lack of interest and expertise of AID field officers with labor projects has a bureaucratic explanation. Typically, "AID missions don't have labor reporting officers on staff," the officer explained, "so they don't have a bureaucratic interest in labor or an understanding of it."[34]

On the other hand, according to this officer, "The State Department is really interested in labor programs, even more than AID in a lot of ways."[35] Likewise, the AID-contracted evaluation of AIFLD mentioned earlier found country-level links between AIFLD and U.S. embassies to be tight. "In a number, and probably most, AID Missions," the evaluating team reported, "the AIFLD program is regarded as a political operation more appropriately a concern of the Embassy and particularly the labor attaché or labor reporting officer."[36]

At the embassies themselves, the evaluating team found that not only labor attachés and reporting officers were interested. "Ambassadors and chargés also seemed to view the labor situation as one of the critical aspects in the political-social-economic context. AIFLD is viewed as a source of information, an entrée to meet influential people and a factor that could affect U.S. interests in promoting free democratic trade unions."[37] Richard Whitaker confirms the same pattern regarding the Asian institute's labor projects. "Embassies have labor reporting officers and labor attachés on staff, and AAFLI gives them entrée to labor groups in-country," he explained.[38]

Holding the AFL-CIO accountable for its government-funded labor projects is also hampered by a pattern of secrecy and obstructionism in the institutes themselves. The labor institutes do not publicize the destination of all their funding, nor do they reveal details concerning many of their programs. In response to an inquiry requesting information about AAFLI's programs, its country priorities as defined by funding levels, and similar topics, AAFLI's program officer responded that the institute is "a technical assistance program, not a clearinghouse for information on the trade union situation in Asia."[39] Likewise, despite repeated requests from the author that were funneled through a U.S. senator's office, the Asian institute stonewalled on producing annual reports, suggesting that such documents were not public information. Annual reports from both AAFLI and AIFLD, requested through a variety of labor and governmental agencies, were never provided to the author through official channels.

A hush-hush attitude surrounds controversial institute programs as well. In its 1989 programs in Nicaragua, the Free Trade Union Institute did not want to identify to NED either the activities planned or the organizational beneficiaries of its NED-funded humanitarian assistance programs.[40] The endowment settled for a statement from FTUI on the number of families served by the programs. In previous years, FTUI secretly funneled grants to programs in Panama that bolstered the candidacy of the military-backed contender in the 1984 presidential elections. It also secretly funded unionists in France who opposed Socialist president François Mitterand in elections there.

Likewise, in a memorandum to the president of NED, Eugenia Kemble, then the executive director of FTUI, listed several countries in which she wanted details on budgets and programs to be kept under wraps.[41] These countries included Chile, Brazil, Nicaragua, Poland, France, Portugal, Suriname, Paraguay, and the Philippines. The resulting secrecy was not confined to Congress or the U.S. public, apparently. In the mid-1980s Joseph Lee, the U.S. embassy's labor attaché in the Philippines, inquired into the use of NED grants by AAFLI in that country. He was told by the State Department to "lay off." Irving Brown, then director of the AFL-CIO's Department of International Affairs, blocked Lee's inquiries and threatened to have him fired if he continued his investigations.[42]

Behind Closed Doors

In keeping with this pattern of secrecy in the AFL-CIO's international operations, decision-making regarding the choice of priorities and the general thrust of institute programs occurs in the shadows of the AFL-CIO's executive offices and its International Affairs Department (popularly known as the DIA). As one top level staff member of the international affairs department of a major U.S. union said in an interview, "The decision-making process in the whole AFL-CIO complex is a bit inscrutable, it's cryptic." Intimate links between the AFL-CIO's executive officers, the DIA, and top levels of the institutes facilitate this back-room policy-making and planning. Decisions made at these high levels are then passed down to field staff for implementation.

Technically, each of the institutes is governed by a board of directors headed by the president and secretary-treasurer of the AFL-CIO and composed primarily of the presidents of major U.S. unions.[43] This structure means that the conservative AFL-CIO hierarchy dominates the institutes. Because AFL-CIO President Lane Kirkland is president of the board of each of the institutes, he can act as gatekeeper in terms of the type of material presented at board meetings and the manner of its presentation. Even more significantly, Kirkland nominates the executive directors of the institutes, and his choices—in the words of one union international affairs staff official—are invariably "rubberstamped" by institute board members.

These executive officers are central to the policy choices and program directions of the institutes. In fact, the executive and regional offices of the institutes are far more important in determining the character of country programs than are the boards which purportedly govern the institutes.[44] A staff person for a major industrial union who used to work in the union's international affairs department said that the boards of the institutes are "not very important or influential at all."[45] This author was told, for instance, that AIFLD board members generally first receive their copies of institute annual reports—usually containing a substantial number of pages—during the board meetings. The reports are handed out by Kirkland or some other top official and are voted on without allowing the board members adequate time to review the documents or investigate the activities they describe.

The senior staff of the executive offices, on the other hand, were described by one evaluating team as "operational." In addition to overseeing the operations of the institutes, they network with foreign governments, AID country missions, U.S. embassies, and Congress.[46] In AIFLD's case, the senior executive staff are credited with formulating various foreign policy initiatives, including conceiving labor's role in the Caribbean Basin Initiative and generating the concept of the tripartite Central American Development Organization to oversee economic aid distribution in the region.[47]

Through their funding relationships with AFL-CIO affiliates in this country, the institutes' top staff members influence personnel selection for the international affairs departments of some recipient unions here in the United States.[48] Not all U.S. unions have such departments, primarily because they do not have the resources to fund such activities. Most of those that do have international affairs departments get most of their funding from the AFL-CIO's international institutes. According to one former top staff member in the international affairs department of a major industrial union, the institutes often have veto power over the choice of the top staff persons in the unions' DIAs. Moreover, the institutes generally "recommend" personnel to fill those positions.

One particularly glaring example concerns the Service Employees International Union (SEIU). Immediately after receiving institute funding for its international affairs department, the SEIU created a position for an Assistant Director of International Affairs. Martin Doherty, son of AIFLD head William Doherty, was brought in to fill the slot. Martin—like many of the other bureaucrats in the institutes—had no trade union background. He had been a Peace Corps worker in Ecuador. The SEIU's director of international affairs, Martin Forrester, had been a labor attaché but, like Doherty, had no trade union background.

The Bricklayers Union is a "classic example" of this phenomenon, according to one influential union staffer. The Bricklayers "didn't think of anything outside of New Jersey" until the National Endowment for Democracy was created, this staff member said. Then Joel Freedman, a member of the rightwing Social Democrats USA (SD/USA) and a participant in the Freedom House Working Group on Central America, was picked to be international affairs adviser to union head Jack Joyce. Freedman, the staffer explained, was tapped by Carl Gershman—president of NED, member of SD/USA, and formerly with Freedom House—to act as adviser to Joyce, who now sits on NED's board.

According to a variety of unionists, each of whom asked to remain anonymous, a small clique of individuals in the International Affairs Department drive the AFL-CIO's foreign policy. These influential figures work closely with Lane Kirkland, Thomas Donahue—secretary-treasurer of the AFL-CIO, Kirkland's top assistants, and institute executives. Known for its hard-line anticommunism, the department is the operating arm of the AFL-CIO in questions of foreign policy. The department coordinates the international efforts of the labor federation and oversees the work of the regional institutes.

The DIA is headed by Tom Kahn, an anticommunist ideologue who had no trade union background until he joined the AFL-CIO's bureaucracy. He is the bridge between the department and the group surrounding Kirkland. Acting as a "staff insider" with influence reaching up to the AFL-CIO's executive council and out to the institutes,

Kahn has become a "real power" in the decision-making apparatus of the AFL-CIO, according to one union activist. Kahn's influence in the institutes is magnified by his position on the board of directors of the Free Trade Union Institute, the funnel for millions of dollars of government money to each of the other institutes. In addition, his assistant in the DIA, Paul Somogyi, took over as executive director of FTUI in 1990.

The department provides a centralized contact point for interactions with government agencies and international organizations on questions of foreign policy. It maintains links with the State Department, the Department of Labor, AID, and the U.S. Information Agency. It also coordinates the AFL-CIO's involvement in the Trade Union Advisory Committee of the Organization for Economic Cooperation and Development, the International Confederation of Free Trade Unions, and the International Labor Organization. These international policy-making and labor advocacy bodies serve as conduits for the AFL-CIO's conservative and probusiness unionism.

The department also wields influence because the ideologues in charge there control the agenda and frame the debate within the top decision-making levels of the labor federation. As an example, the DIA cranks out position papers on foreign policy and floats resolutions to the AFL-CIO executive council. The executive council—composed of Kirkland, Donahue, and about 30 presidents and vice-presidents of major unions—is responsible for setting overall AFL-CIO policy between the biannual AFL-CIO conventions. It also presents resolutions to convention delegates during convention years which, when voted on, become the public policy of the labor federation.

The executive council's subcommittee on international affairs reviews the DIA's papers and resolutions. But the subcommittee's capacity to give adequate consideration to and feedback on a given issue varies widely, depending on the participants' level of interest and knowledge, the amount of information readily available on the issue, and whether there are staff members available to the subcommittee members for background research and advice. In addition, the committees and subcommittees attached to the federation are themselves sometimes headed by conservative ideologues. The AFL-CIO's Committee on Defense, for example, is chaired by John T. Joyce. Similarly, the executive council's subcommittee on *perestroika* is headed by Albert Shanker of the American Federation of Teachers. Because of these structural features, the DIA—by controlling the general framework of the policy discussion—has substantial weight in the policy-making process.

In conversations with unionists and labor analysts, it was impossible to get a firm grip on the exact relationship of these top level labor bureaucrats to the State Department, CIA, and other policy-making and operational arms of the U.S. government. The secrecy surrounding the AFL-CIO's foreign policy decision-making process means that such links are well-concealed. So too is the direction of influence—whether from the AFL-CIO to the government, or the other way around. As one unionist said, "It's hard enough to expose the nature of and contradictions in the AFL-CIO's foreign policy, but explaining where policy comes from and why it is the way it is can only probably be answered by getting inside the heads of these people."

Historical Partnership

Because organized labor's involvement in international affairs goes back a long way, explaining the AFL-CIO's foreign policy is in part a historical task. Even back as far as 1881, the Federation of Organized Trades and Labor Unions of the United States and Canada— forerunner to the AFL—passed a resolution protesting the "conditions of the oppressed people" of Ireland.[49] At its 1896 convention, the AFL endorsed the struggle of the Cuban revolutionaries, with Samuel Gompers asserting the need for Cuban independence from Spain as a prerequisite to organizing workers on the island.

Gompers, who helped found the AFL and headed the organization until his death in 1924, was a zealous internationalist who established the guiding principles of the labor federation's foreign policy.[50] Gompers was anti-colonial, but he did not oppose U.S. expansionism if outright territorial acquisition was not the objective. On the contrary, he approved the gradual, non-military extension of U.S. commerce and influence around the world. "The nation which dominates the markets of the world will surely control its destinies," he told the Anti-Imperialist League in 1898. In the same speech he urged the United States not to annex the Philippines, arguing that "neither its gates nor those of any other country of the globe can long be closed against our constantly growing industrial supremacy."[51] By the turn of the century, the AFL backed the gradual enlargement of the U.S. sphere of influence, while formally disavowing U.S. annexations of the spoils of the Spanish-American War, including Cuba, Puerto Rico, and the Philippines.[52]

These early years of the AFL were not marked by any special closeness with Washington. The federation was then preoccupied with pulling itself together as a unified body, a process that involved purging radical elements or diluting their influence. Domestic matters and organizational requirements were far more important than international affairs in terms of occupying labor's time and resources. Support for or opposition to U.S. foreign policy were acted out in the battle for public opinion and in vote mobilizations during electoral campaigns.

But the erosion of U.S. labor militancy—spurred by Gompers' growing belief in business unionism, government support for AFL unions, repression of leftwing unions, and increasing affluence in the United States—gradually tightened the bonds between the AFL and Washington.[53] At the turn of the century sharp divisions existed between politically radical elements of the U.S. labor movement such as the Industrial Workers of the World (IWW) and more conservative associations, such as the American Federation of Labor. Government suppression of the IWW in favor of the American Federation of Labor during World War I cleared the playing field of many of U.S. labor's most militant factions.

The general contours of the modern-day alliance between organized labor and the U.S. government were forged during World War I under Gompers. In a departure from the labor internationalism which had characterized both the leftwing and procapitalist union movements until that time, the war inflamed nationalist sentiments among workers around the world. In the United States, Gompers engineered a mutual-support deal with Washington, delivering a loyal and disciplined workforce in exchange for government recognition of its right to organize.

Following the war, the AFL continued to receive government assistance for overseas activities despite being buffeted by a government-backed corporate crackdown on its domestic union activities. A secret 1918 injection of $50,000 from the administration of Woodrow Wilson, for instance, financed the creation of the Pan-American Labor Press, a publication intended to advocate the establishment of the Pan-American Federation of Labor.[54] A brainchild of Samuel Gompers, the federation was designed to extend U.S. economic and political influence throughout Latin America.[55] Gompers himself described it as "based upon the spirit of the Monroe Doctrine."

Although the organization never really got off the ground, it illustrated the U.S. federation's empire-building approach to Latin American labor, an approach which has been carried out not only in that region but around the world over the past half century. Reflecting these criticisms, labor activist Santiago Iglesias in 1927 condemned the Pan-American federation as the "child of the American Federation of Labor" and the "instrumentality" through which radical Latin American unions, inspired by the revolution in the Soviet Union, would be controlled. The Pan-American federation, Iglesias insisted, was a product of Gompers' vanity and wish to shield the United States and its Latin American sphere of influence from radical unionism.[56]

By the beginning of World War II, the American Federation of Labor—which had not yet merged with the Congress of Industrial Organizations—was positioned to become deeply involved as an operations arm of U.S. foreign policy. Although both federations had offices and operations in Europe, it was the more conservative AFL that was closely tied to Washington both politically and financially.[57] The AFL coordinated its war effort with Washington and with allies overseas through its International Affairs Department, created at the onset of the war, and through the Free Trade Union Committee, established in 1944. These entities in turn cooperated with the Office of Strategic Services (OSS—precursor to the CIA) in programs in Europe, Africa, and Asia.

From the beginning, the international affairs department and the Free Trade Union Committee (FTUC) were wedded to a militant anticommunism which aligned them neatly with the long-term political objectives of Washington. The department of international affairs, for example, was run by anti-communist stalwarts such as Matthew Woll, David Dubinsky, and Jay Lovestone. Lovestone, of course, was a key figure in these early years, acting first as executive secretary of the FTUC and later as head of the international affairs department. Dubinsky and Woll were as committed as Lovestone to anticommunism as a foundation of the AFL's foreign policy. Dubinsky, head of the Ladies' Garment Workers' Union and once a socialist himself, came to oppose communism both in principle and because of infighting in his union. Woll, of the Photoengravers' union, was the former president of the National Civic Federation, an association of employers and conservative unionists funded by top U.S. industrialists and financiers.[58]

Drawing on its solid links to U.S. government agencies, the AFL stepped into the postwar vacuum of war-devastated Europe. It became an ardent backer of the Marshall Plan and mounted a CIA-funded struggle for control of European trade union movements.[59] The European labor arena during the immediate postwar years was the site of an intense Cold War competition for the region's workers. Communist unions and leftwing social movements, their legitimacy enhanced by years of resistance to Europe's fascist dictatorships, faced off against U.S.-backed unionists intent on achieving ideological and institutional dominance in European labor movements.

Labor leaders from the United States—funded by U.S. corporations and the CIA and supported by the State Department and U.S. embassies—were instrumental in these efforts. They financed organizing and propaganda activities, selected candidates to lead foreign unions, financed their campaigns, paid off supporters, and helped build pro-western union infrastructures. The Free Trade Union Committee, created to "help [foreign] unions resist the new drives of totalitarian forces," acted both during and after the war as a branch of U.S. intelligence operations to win the battle for these unions. Through top operatives such as Irving Brown, funds from government, corporations, and unions were funneled to conservative and Christian Democratic trade unions in Europe.

In France, Brown helped finance and organize a breakaway union to oppose the country's major federation, the communist-dominated General Confederation of Labor (CGT). He also chose "competent militants" to run the new organization, the Force Ouvrière (Workers Force), which continues to receive U.S. support from the National Endowment for Democracy for projects in Africa and the Caribbean.[60] Italy and Greece also were targeted, and in Germany the AFL decided which unions and labor leaders would receive preferential treatment from the Allied occupation forces. The litmus test used to select such beneficiaries was based on the unionists' beliefs regarding the Soviet Union, not on their records of opposing the Nazis or the firmness of their commitment to workers.[61]

The U.S. federation's relationship with government was so tight during these years that AFL President George Meany headed an interagency labor advisory program that coordinated international projects relating to trade unions. This interagency office operated out of the State Department.[62] The AFL was given control over selections of labor attachés for U.S. embassies around the world and approved delegations of trade unionists to and from the United States.

The U.S. federation was also active in the third world during the immediate postwar period. In Africa, the AFL pursued various activities through the new International Confederation of Free Trade Unions (ICFTU), an international organization of anticommunist union federations set up in 1949. Through the ICFTU, the U.S. federation backed union newsletters and magazines, provided institutional support, and supported trainings, especially when these activities had an anti-colonial focus. The federation dropped out of the ICFTU from 1952 to 1953, however, accusing the organization of lacking sufficient commitment to anticommunism and of being soft on colonialism. As a consequence of these rocky relations, the federation continued to emphasize unilateral aid programs initially set up by the Office of Strategic Services and the Free Trade Union Committee. By 1955—with the merger of the American Federation of Labor and the Congress of Industrial Organizations and following more troubled relations with the international confederation and its member unions—the AFL-CIO set up its own African regional fund.[63]

The labor federation threw its weight behind African movements for decolonization, in the process pitting itself against union federations from colonial powers such as Britain and France.[64] From the beginning, however, these struggles had an anticommunist focus and a pro-U.S. agenda. Labor leaders like Tom Mboya in Kenya, for example, were supported because of their sympathies with Washington, their amenability to U.S. corporate involvement in their countries, and the alternatives they offered to leftwing unions.[65]

In Asia, the anticommunist agenda was even more prominent during the early postwar years. There, the AFL worked to shore up allied governments in Korea, the Philippines, and Indonesia following the 1949 communist victory in China. Similarly, projects undertaken in Turkey had the strategic objective of bolstering a friendly government on NATO's eastern flank.[66] From an initial focus on training projects, the U.S. labor federation's programs expanded to include social service projects and union-building activities designed to counteract appeals from communist unions. In some cases, as in Korea and South Vietnam, the U.S. labor's programs dovetailed with military pacification and counterrevolutionary activities.[67]

During the 1940s and 1950s, the Latin American programs of U.S. labor were coordinated by Serafino Romualdi, a representative of the International Ladies' Garment Workers' Union who had worked as an agent for the Office of Strategic Services. After several years of networking and creating linkages between conservative unionists in Latin America and the United States, Romualdi moved—with State Department assistance—to organize a conservative counterweight to nationalist Latin American union movements. Known since 1951 as the Interamerican Regional Organization of Workers (ORIT), the regional confederation Romualdi helped construct has generally provided strong support to U.S. foreign policy in the region.[68] It also has offered an important avenue of access to Latin American unions for the AFL-CIO. Since the 1960s, however, the AFL-CIO's programs in Latin America have been dominated by AIFLD, although union-to-union programs through international trade secretariats and ORIT are still vital components of U.S. labor's presence in the region.

CHAPTER TWO
Enlisting in the Reagan-Bush "Democracy" Offensive

Regardless of the secrecy surrounding their activities, the AFL-CIO's international institutes are clearly key players in a larger network of interlocking private organizations and government agencies that help promote Washington's foreign policy. Using U.S. government funds and logistical assistance, these organizations intervene overseas with the purported objective of promoting democracy. The National Endowment for Democracy (NED) is the current centerpiece of this bipartisan, "democracy-intervention" network. Members of this network range from humanitarian assistance organizations like the International Rescue Committee to anticommunist propaganda institutions such as Freedom House.

Model for Democracy-Intervention

Ever since World War II, when the AFL-CIO was brought into the war effort as part of a patriotic coalition with Washington and big business, the AFL-CIO has acted as the vanguard of a bipartisan "democracy-building" strategy that relies on private organizations to carry out certain sensitive government policies overseas. The ultimate goal of that strategy is the extension of the U.S. sphere of influence. Its adherents, however, justify it with a rhetoric of democracy and liberty. Although never phrased so brutishly, their rationale explains U.S. meddling in the domestic affairs of foreign countries as a mission of benevolent goodwill. Adrian Karatnycky of the AFL-CIO's International Affairs Department emphasized those good intentions in an interview with a Unification Church-owned publication in 1988. "Where we are, I think," Karatnycky told *Insight* magazine, "is where most American workers are, which is trying to advance a foreign policy that is well-aware that America is the principal force for democracy in the world."[1]

41

Labor, along with business and the two U.S. political parties, is one of four strategic sectors represented in this democracy-intervention network. In fact, the AFL-CIO's international institutes were used as a model for both structural and tactical elements of the "democracy-building" activities of the past decade. Although there were other models as well—like the Inter-American Foundation and the Asia Foundation—the AFL-CIO and its labor institutes have been especially important because of the global network managed by these organizations and because of the strategic importance of access to and influence over foreign labor. As AFL-CIO President Lane Kirkland put it in arguing for the establishment of the National Endowment for Democracy, labor had "the longest track record on the international scene" of all the private organizations which helped formulate NED and the new democracy-building strategy.[2]

A key feature of the model is the participation of both governmental and nongovernmental representatives and—on the private side—the cooperation of both business and labor on major policy issues. The labor federation has had a long history of participating in such tripartite (government-business-labor) activities. AFL representatives served on the National Civic Federation at the turn of the century, for instance, and the AFL also participated with government and business on war production boards during World War II. Later, the AFL-CIO worked with corporate and government leaders to formulate the Alliance for Progress programs of the 1960s. Today, NED's directors include representatives of big business and organized labor, as well as political party leaders and former government officials.

In addition to these structural features, the AFL-CIO offered a template for tactical activities of the democracy-intervention movement. William E. Brock, one of the principal figures involved in formulating NED, lauded the institutes as some of the "best known" of the models used to design the endowment. The aid they offer to "free labor unions," Brock said, "has been one of the most effective tools the U.S. has possessed in the postwar period to halt the spread of communism through subversion of workers' movements in the developing world."[3] Institution-building activities such as trainings, personnel subsidies, media projects, social service programs, and infrastructure-development are all projects first carried out by labor which are now implemented by members of the broader intervention network with their own constituencies.

Members of the labor federation even helped construct the framework of the recent democracy-intervention movement. Top labor figures, for example, participated in the National Bipartisan Commission on Central America (Kissinger Commission), which recommended that the United States put greater emphasis on building friendly foreign institutions in its regional foreign policy. AFL-CIO head Lane Kirkland was a member of the commission, while William Doherty was a key consultant.

AFL-CIO principals also helped design the National Endowment for Democracy. Both Lane Kirkland and Eugenia Kemble—then an assistant to Albert Shanker, president of the American Federation of Teachers—worked with the American Political Foundation on the Democracy Program. Funded by the Reagan administration, the Democracy Program recommended establishing NED. It also advocated using the AFL-CIO's nearly defunct Free Trade Union Institute as NED's core grantee for labor grants.

From 1984 to 1990, NED received more than $152 million from the U.S. government to support its "democracy-building" efforts. A grant-making institution, NED has channeled aid to an extensive network of private organizations working in more than 100 countries around the world.

NED's grants—like those of the AFL-CIO's labor institutes—are designed to strengthen pro-U.S. organizations and promote a positive view of U.S. foreign policy overseas. It has used government funds to back political parties, business associations, trade unions, women's and youth groups, media projects, and partisan political activities in countries ranging from Mexico to Indonesia, and from Portugal to South Africa.

The endowment's four core grantees represent major political sectors in the United States: labor, business, and the two dominant political parties. Along with the AFL-CIO's Free Trade Union Institute, the other core grantees are the Center for International Private Enterprise, National Democratic Institute for International Affairs, and National Republican Institute for International Affairs. The majority of NED's funds are channeled through these core grantees, but other grants are funneled through U.S.-based "discretionary grantees" such as Freedom House and the League for Industrial Democracy.

Following NED's establishment in 1983, Kirkland and Shanker became members of the endowment's board of directors. Kemble stepped in as the executive director of the Free Trade Union Institute. Moreover, the AFL-CIO apparently had the final say over the selection of NED's president, Carl Gershman, a longtime friend of organized labor. Kirkland—who is a director of FTUI—reportedly offered to split some of the labor institute's hefty share of the initial NED appropriation with the political party institutes on the condition that the AFL-CIO hierarchy be given approval rights over who was selected as NED's president.[4]

A Strategic Sector

Private organizations have been an essential element in this postwar intervention network for various reasons. Nongovernmental groups from the United States can penetrate foreign arenas—like trade unions—in which it would be difficult or impossible for the U.S. government to act openly. Moreover, shielded by their private status, these allies of Washington are spared most of the oversight and public scrutiny which would be aimed at similar initiatives if they were carried out by government agencies.

Speaking of Latin America, one set of observers acknowledged the important function private organizations like the AFL-CIO's Latin American institute play in U.S. foreign policy:

> The communist elements [in Latin America] do gain from region wide feelings of nationalism that pit the U.S. against their smaller, more economically dependent neighbors to the south. Current international debt crises and the austerity measures recommended by the IMF with U.S. support are used to generate [anti-U.S. government] feelings on the part of workers. The role that U.S. multinational corporations are perceived to have played in the development process reinforces these views. This is a major reason why the AF of L-CIO is a better vehicle as a fraternal organization to promote free democratic trade unions than direct U.S. government involvement.[5]

In other words, the federation and its institutes are useful fronts for the U.S. government when it comes to international labor sectors that distrust official U.S. initiatives. By capitalizing on its fraternal status as an organization of workers, the AFL-CIO can actually help to further U.S. interests that compete with those of foreign workers. In so doing, the U.S. federation undermines not only communist elements overseas. It also helps counteract those democratic leftwing and nationalist social forces that oppose economic and political subservience to Washington and austerity measures that balance budgets on the backs of the poor and the working class.

Unionists are particularly important in the geopolitical strategies of the U.S. government because of their political importance and because of the role they play in national economies. In fact, trade unions are so strategically significant that they have been used by governments of all political stripes to penetrate and manipulate foreign political arenas. As a former research director of the International Affairs Department of the United Auto Workers described it,

[G]overnments and political parties have used the international labor movement as one of the principal vehicles for their covert interactions with political parties and governments in foreign nations. The international trades union movement has been, and continues to be, a vital tool of governments in the shaping of the political destinies of foreign political parties and states and is an important part of most nations' foreign-policy systems.[6]

Labor is a strategic sector in U.S. foreign policy because of its organizational characteristics as well. As large, hierarchically structured organizations with access to personnel and money, unions can rapidly mobilize people in support of, or in opposition to, a given regime or set of policies. Roy Godson points to such factors to explain labor's importance in foreign policy. Godson is in a position to know. A member of Reagan's 1980 transition team on intelligence policy, he also worked closely with the AFL-CIO's CIA-linked Free Trade Union Committee and the American Institute for Free Labor Development.[7]

Godson—whose father Joseph was a senior consultant to the Democracy Program study—notes that labor-backed mobilizations are particularly important in strategic sectors of the economy. Breakdowns in any one of these sectors—for example, transportation, communications, energy, or public services—can immobilize an entire society. On the other hand, as in the 1973 CIA-backed coup in Chile, strategically placed U.S.-backed labor operatives in sectors such as communications and transportation can keep essential lines of communication open and facilitate the overthrow of elected governments by reactionary militaries.

Trade unions can use their numbers to undermine or to reinforce the stability of a political system, alter the political balance of a country through coalition-formation or withdrawal, and challenge or defend public policies. In the past decade, for example, U.S.-funded labor federations in Chile, El Salvador, the Philippines, Nicaragua, and Poland mobilized their members to elect U.S.-backed candidates and defeat those opposed by Washington. Likewise, the anticommunist Bulgarian union federation, Podkrepa, backed by the U.S. government with AID and USIA funds, precipitated country-wide strikes during November 1990 which eventually led to the downfall of the government.[8]

Trade unions also provide avenues by which the United States may penetrate wider political sectors abroad. Often unionists are key access points to political parties and social groups, as well as being agents of influence within national labor organizations. This is especially true in Africa and Asia, where postwar anti-colonial battles linked unions and political parties against foreign domination. It is also the case in Eastern Europe, where loose alliances of workers and intellectuals helped topple ossified communist regimes. The long-term backing provided by NED through FTUI to the Solidarity trade union in Poland, for instance, gave the United States access to top government officials in the Solidarity governments under Tadeusz Mazowiecki and his successor, Lech Walesa.

Interventionist Network

During the 1980s, the Cold War battlefield widened to include the overt deployment of explicitly political and ideological weapons. As a result of this shift, the AFL-CIO's international operations received a boost from NED. Using NED funds, the international institutes of the AFL-CIO have been able to expand their political activities overseas. At the same time, relying on government funding from other agencies, the institutes have continued to back the union-building and social service projects that have attracted foreign workers to their programs over the years. NED's support has thus enhanced the AFL-CIO's already formidable role as a component of the U.S. foreign policy apparatus, with both political and economic influence over strategic labor sectors overseas.

Various interconnections exist between the endowment and the labor institutes. Over the years, the Free Trade Union Institute has shared three directors—Albert Shanker, Lane Kirkland, and John T. Joyce—with NED. Representatives from the other three labor institutes sit on FTUI's board, which in turn funnels endowment grants to those institutes. Moreover, some FTUI directors are associated with other endowment grantees. They have included John DeConcini (A. Philip Randolph Institute), John Joyce (National Democratic Institute for International Affairs, A. Philip Randolph Institute, League for Industrial Democracy, Friends of the Democratic Center in Central America), and Tom Kahn.

Like other top leaders of the AFL-CIO, Tom Kahn is affiliated with various organizations that form an anticommunist phalanx with U.S. foreign policy influence. Kahn, who heads the federation's powerful international affairs department, is a principal of Social Democrats USA (SD/USA). A small, self-described social democratic organization, SD/USA's policies and activities dovetail smartly with U.S. interventionism abroad, and its leaders dominate the foreign policy apparatus of the AFL-CIO. Largely composed of ex-Trotskyites, the organization is a rightwing breakaway faction from the U.S. Socialist Party, which split over conceptions of the proper role for the United

States to play in Vietnam. Through the strategic placement of members such as Carl Gershman and Tom Kahn, SD/USA has exercised a profound influence in the export of anticommunist ideology and U.S. influence under the guise of promoting democracy. But as one top union staffer explained, the organization is "not only anticommunist, but anti-left," a fact that strictly limits its alliances around the world.

In the 1970s, under the leadership of Carl Gershman, SD/USA became a supporter of Senator Henry (Scoop) Jackson and his contingent of hawkish "defenders of democracy." Working with Jackson, SD/USA's members gained political experience but little political power. With the election of Ronald Reagan in 1980, however, key figures in SD/USA achieved positions of power and influence both in the labor movement and in the government.[9] Among the latter were Reagan era appointees such as United Nations Ambassador Jeane Kirkpatrick, Assistant Secretary of State for Inter-American Affairs Elliott Abrams, and Geneva arms talks negotiator Max Kampelman.

Under the Bush administration, SD/USA has lost its high profile representatives in government. It continues to dominate the AFL-CIO's foreign policy, however. Its members are frequently staffers or officers of the institutes and the AFL-CIO's international affairs department. They perform operational and decision-making functions, working behind the scenes to plan and implement policy. Besides Kahn, influential SD/USA members in U.S. labor include Albert Shanker, Adrian Karatnycky, Eugenia Kemble, and David Jessup (AIFLD Special Assistant). Joel Freedman, married to SD/USA's national secretary Rita Freedman, worked as international affairs adviser to John Joyce with funding from the NED.[10]

In addition to his membership in SD/USA, Kahn is the former executive director of the League for Industrial Democracy. The League is a conservative labor advocacy organization which shares offices with and is influenced by SD/USA and has received funding from the National Endowment for Democracy. Kahn also serves on the boards of the NED-funded A. Philip Randolph Institute, International Rescue Committee, Committee in Support of Solidarity, and Institute for Democracy in Eastern Europe. He is a member of the American Federation of Teachers, which also receives NED grants. Along with William Doherty of the American Institute for Free Labor Development, Kahn sits on the board of the Inter-American Foundation, a grant-making agency established and funded by Congress to promote Latin American development projects. The foundation, long known for funding progressive programs, suffered a shake-up under the Reagan administration and shifted in a more conservative direction in the 1980s.

Lane Kirkland straddles both the government and private sectors, exemplifying the interconnections between the two which character- ize the intervention network. AFL-CIO President since 1979, Kirkland served on the board of the American Political Foundation and has been a director of NED since 1983. As AFL-CIO president, he automatically serves as president of the Free Trade Union Institute, American Insti- tute for Free Labor Development, Asian-American Free Labor Institute, and African-American Labor Center. He was a member of the Council on Foreign Relations and the Atlantic Council, two think tanks which helped shape postwar foreign policy in the United States. He also served on the board of the U.S. Information Agency's Radio Free Europe/Radio Liberty and was a founder of the rightwing Committee on the Present Danger.

Kirkland has been tapped by presidents of both political parties to participate on government-sponsored commissions and panels, with a special emphasis on economic and foreign policy issues. For instance, he was a member of the Kissinger Commission under the Reagan administration and a member of the Commission on Financial Structure and the Blue Ribbon Defense Commission under Richard Nixon. He served on the Commission on CIA Activities in the mid- 1970s and later joined the Commission on the National Agenda for the 1980s under President Jimmy Carter. He has also been a member of the General Advisory Committee of the Arms Control and Disarmament Agency.

Freedom House is one of the most influential "democracy-build- ing" havens for labor activists, particularly those affiliated with Social Democrats USA. Advertised as a documentation center and clearing- house on human and civil rights, Freedom House is a neoconservative heavyweight in the global war of ideas. During the postwar period, it has provided exhaustive "documentation" of human rights abuses by Soviet and leftist governments, while downplaying and under-report- ing abuses in U.S.-allied countries.

From 1984 to 1990, Freedom House funneled some $4.1 million from NED to overseas grant recipients, primarily for "informational" projects. Freedom House grants sometimes overlap with NED's grants to the labor institutes. For example, both Freedom House and AIFLD used NED funds to support the anti-Sandinista publications house, Libro Libre, in Costa Rica. Similarly, in the May/June 1988 issue of its journal *Freedom at Issue,* Freedom House printed an article about education under Nicaragua's Sandinista "dictatorship." The article resulted from a NED-funded study conducted by the American Feder- ation of Teachers and was widely distributed by that federation and AIFLD.[11]

In 1988, Freedom House sponsored a ten-member Working Group on Central America which included AIFLD's executive director William Doherty. Among other things, the group suggested that Washington funnel "political aid" to the political opposition facing the Sandinistas in the 1990 elections while simultaneously maintaining the "cohesion" of the contras. Another member of the Working Group was Penn Kemble, a member of Social Democrats USA and brother of FTUI's first executive director, Eugenia Kemble. Penn Kemble was one of the so-called "Gang of Four" Democrats who helped persuade Congress to funnel aid to the Nicaraguan contras in 1986.[12] He is now a director of the NED-funded National Democratic Institute for International Affairs. Top unionists who are members of the board of trustees at Freedom House include Albert Shanker, William Doherty, Sol C. Chaikin, and Norman Hill. NED's president and staunch labor ally Carl Gershman once worked as a Freedom House scholar.

A variety of other NED grantees known for their politicized activities also include members of the U.S. labor leadership among their directors. As mentioned above, Tom Kahn sits on the boards of the Committee in Support of Solidarity and the Institute for Democracy in Eastern Europe. These organizations funneled U.S. government funds to dissident groups in Eastern Europe prior to the downfall of the region's communist governments. Their grants are now used to provide infrastructure support, produce and distribute publications, and assist other activities of political organizations in Bulgaria, Czechoslovakia, Hungary, Poland, Romania, and Yugoslavia. During the first six months of 1990 alone, for example, the Institute for Democracy in Eastern Europe received more than $1 million from NED for various projects in Eastern Europe.

Another NED grantee that includes labor leaders on its board is the International Rescue Committee (IRC). A CIA-linked organization, the IRC uses U.S. government funds to channel humanitarian aid to target groups in geopolitical hotspots.[13] In the last decade, it has received grants from both AID and NED to work in such countries as Vietnam, Cambodia, El Salvador, Honduras, Afghanistan, and Poland. In July 1990 three top representatives of the IRC accompanied an AFL-CIO delegation of state federation presidents to a Cambodian refugee camp to inaugurate a Khmer women's agricultural training project.[14] Carl Gershman, Tom Kahn, Albert Shanker, and Jay Mazur of the AFL-CIO Executive Council have all served as directors of the committee.

William Doherty and John T. Joyce were board members of PRODEMCA (Friends of the Democratic Center in Central America). A NED grantee for anti-Sandinista projects inside Nicaragua, the organization was headed by Penn Kemble. PRODEMCA was described by Aryeh Neier of Americas Watch, a human rights watchdog group, as the "kiss of death for independent organizations inside Nicaragua."[15] While receiving grants from the endowment, PRODEMCA used funds generated from Oliver North's illegal contra support and drug-running network to launch media campaigns in the United States in support of military aid to the Nicaraguan contras. The group also conducted free tours of a contra base camp in Honduras for selected policy makers, journalists, and academics who were thought influential in the contra aid debate. A congressional source told the *Washington Post* that the camp was "basically there to put on a dog-and-pony show for visiting congressional delegations. It's a carefully controlled atmosphere. The people they are allowed to talk to will give the party line."[16]

Another group with ties to organized labor in the United States is the League for Industrial Democracy (LID). The league was established in 1905 to educate students and other members of society about socialist principles of democracy and labor. Over the years it lost its progressive orientation and by the 1950s became involved with the CIA in efforts to combat communism.[17] Now dominated by anticommunists, its board is composed primarily of neoconservatives associated with the Social Democrats USA and the international institutes of the AFL-CIO.

Included among LID ranks are Sol Chaikin, Eric Chenowith, William Doherty, Evelyn Dubrow, Larry Dugan, Jr., Norman Hill, David Jessup, John T. Joyce, Tom Kahn, Jay Mazur, Joyce Miller, Albert Shanker, Donald Slaiman, John J. Sweeney, and Lynn R. Williams. Penn Kemble and Roy Godson, a specialist in labor and intelligence theory, are also LID directors. The league received a NED grant in 1985 "for a study on the interrelationship between democratic trade unions and political parties, with special emphasis on socialist and social democratic parties, to examine their attitudes toward U.S. labor, foreign-policy, [and] economic issues."[18]

AIFLD's Agent for All Seasons

A key figure in the international activities of the AFL-CIO has been William C. Doherty, Jr. Executive director of AIFLD since 1965, he has guided AIFLD's development as a conservative, anticommunist, probusiness labor institute. According to former intelligence agents, Doherty has also been a crucial link between the U.S. labor sector and the CIA.

Doherty catapulted into the ranks of top U.S. labor leaders shortly after receiving a philosophy degree from Catholic University in 1949.[19] He worked first as an assistant administrator for the Marshall Plan but within a year of graduation was voted president of the American Federation of Government Employees, one of the largest public employee unions in the United States. Following that posting, he went to Europe to work as the assistant director of the regional activities department for the International Confederation of Free Trade Unions. He later worked in South America as the inter-American representative for the Postal, Telegraph, and Telephone International (PTTI), an international trade secretariat through which the CIA ran operations.

In 1962 Doherty became the director of social projects for AIFLD. He assumed the position of executive director of the labor institute in 1965, following the retirement of Serafino Romualdi.

Doherty's father, William C. Doherty, Sr., the longtime president of the letter carriers association, served as a vice-president of the AFL-CIO and as U.S. ambassador to Jamaica. The elder Doherty—his personal expenses paid by the CIA—was identified by former CIA operatives as a conduit for passing intelligence agency funds to foreign union leaders.[20]

Doherty, Jr. apparently followed in his father's footsteps. Philip Agee, a former CIA officer whose exposé *Inside the Company* was described by the CIA as "complete" and "accurate," identified Doherty as a "CIA agent in labor operations."[21] As an agent and organizer, Doherty has been all over Latin America and the Caribbean. He helped form the Interamerican Regional Organization of Workers (ORIT) unions in Honduras during the 1950s and helped coordinate labor operations after U.S. military and electoral successes in Latin America. For example, the U.S. military flew Doherty into Grenada while the invasion was still underway in October 1983, and AIFLD immediately began a training program there aimed at strengthening pro-U.S. unions.[22]

A U.S. government interagency team's December 1983 report explained the importance of AIFLD's presence in Grenada following the overthrow of Maurice Bishop's government. "Organized labor is in disarray now that the dominant, highly radicalized portion of its leadership has been removed," the report observed. Noting that the "radical" unionists had been rounded up or killed along with Bishop, the report pointed out that the U.S. institute had stayed in contact with unions "that can be considered democratic" during Bishop's tenure. "AIFLD is on the scene now," the report continued, and "is developing an extensive plan to reorient and train the labor leadership." It went on to urge AIFLD to assume a leadership role in restructuring Grenada's unions.[23]

Doherty and other top AIFLD staff members visited Nicaragua in mid-1990 during critical, wide-scale anti-government strikes by Sandinista unionists. The AIFLD functionaries gave guidance to anti-Sandinista labor organizations which had used U.S. government funds to back the successful candidacy of Violeta Chamorro during elections the preceding February.

Doherty's involvement in foreign affairs extends beyond his work with the labor institute. He serves on the advisory council of the Inter-American Foundation (IAF), a U.S. government organization which uses AID funds to support development projects in Latin America. Doherty was tapped by the Reagan administration to serve on the advisory committee which sought to replace the IAF's widely respected liberal director with one more compatible with the conservative philosophies of President Reagan and his New Right allies. Doherty also acted as a key consultant to the National Bipartisan Commission on Central America (Kissinger Commission), presenting testimony and proposing recommendations on behalf of the AFL-CIO. He has been an official U.S. election observer in El Salvador, Guatemala, and Honduras.

In addition to these government-backed activities, Doherty has worked with a number of private organizations which focus on foreign policy and labor issues. As noted above, he was a member of the Working Group on Central America sponsored by Freedom House. Doherty was also on the national council of PRODEMCA and is a director of the League for Industrial Democracy.

Doherty headed AIFLD during most of the years that it included business leaders on its board. He found ready allies in corporate partners many would find unlikely friends of labor. "We welcome [the] cooperation [of management] not only financially but in terms of establishing our policies," Doherty has said. "The cooperation between ourselves and the business community is getting warmer day by day."[24]

CHAPTER THREE
Inside the AFL-CIO's
International Program

The AFL-CIO conducts its overseas operations through an apparatus that maximizes its international presence while shielding its activities from public view. This apparatus has two major components. The first consists of the AFL-CIO's four regional institutes. They serve as the primary vehicles through which the AFL-CIO conducts its foreign activities. As specialized organizations, the institutes allow the U.S. federation to tailor its overall foreign policy to specific populations in different regions, while maintaining control over the objectives and content of the programs. Their origins and development are considered in this chapter, while their activities will be covered in the next.

The second major component of the AFL-CIO's international organization is its membership in an assortment of multinational labor bodies. Among them are the International Confederation of Free Trade Unions (ICFTU), the International Labor Organization, and the Trade Union Advisory Committee of the Organization for Economic Cooperation and Development. These multilateral organizations bring together labor, business, and governments from around the world and offer the U.S. federation other significant vehicles to penetrate international arenas and influence foreign affairs. In addition, the international trade secretariats of the ICFTU also serve as important channels of AFL-CIO involvement with foreign unions.

Although the U.S. federation's participation in these multinational bodies is extensive, it is difficult to measure the full effect of the AFL-CIO's influence in them or, through them, on labor sectors overseas. There has been very little in-depth research conducted on most of these organizations, with the exception perhaps of the International Labor Organization and some of the international trade secretariats. Evaluating the effect of each on their target constituencies and measuring the influence of the AFL-CIO on the organizations and on the content of their programs would be fruitful topics for future research. Despite the drawbacks to a complete discussion of this topic in the current volume, it is clear that the U.S. federation considers these multinational bodies important to its overall international objectives. Consequently, after exploring the creation and structure of the regional institutes, this chapter outlines the major features of the AFL-CIO's involvement in several major multilateral bodies in hopes of erecting a framework for more detailed elaboration in the future.

Expanding to Fill a Growing Need

In the immediate postwar period, the AFL-CIO carried out its foreign activities from its Paris office. It focused particularly on consolidating anticommunist union forces in Europe and working with other international and regional bodies like the International Confederation of Free Trade Unions. By the 1960s, however, both Washington and the AFL-CIO felt the need for specialized instruments which could be mobilized by the labor federation for unilateral intervention worldwide. The international institutes of the AFL-CIO were set up to respond to that need.

The Free Trade Union Institute (FTUI), created by the AFL-CIO in 1977, acts both as the European regional institute of the labor federation and as an umbrella for some government grants to the other three institutes. Originally FTUI represented a resuscitated Free Trade Union Committee—the AFL-CIO's European arm during World War II and the postwar years. Following the successful implementation of the Marshall Plan, the committee had gone dormant. When military dictatorships fell in Spain and Portugal in the mid-1970s, the AFL-CIO found itself without an effective apparatus to counter the strong socialist union movements in the two countries. Recognizing the need for an institute that could concentrate on European affairs, the federation went about revitalizing its European arm. As a result, FTUI was established to help prevent communist electoral successes in Spain and Portugal as well as to increase U.S. influence in European trade unions generally.

FTUI's mission was broadened in 1983 to include coordinating and administering labor grants from the National Endowment for Democracy (NED). Now NED's largest grantee, the Free Trade Union Institute disbursed nearly 50 percent of the dollar total of NED's grants from 1984 to 1988. It distributes these NED funds through the other labor institutes, reserving some for its own European grantees. Grants from AID and other government agencies are usually channeled through the other institutes, but a number of AID grants have been designated for FTUI-backed labor organizations in Eastern Europe since the late 1980s.

As the umbrella organization for NED's labor grants, FTUI has served as a conduit for NED funding for projects in countries ranging from Jordan to New Zealand, and from France to Brazil. Its grants support trade union exchanges, civic education, union-building, leadership training, conferences, seminars, and production of trade union publications. It also has assisted trade union exiles and their families and has provided social services for unionists in geopolitical hotspots like Poland.

FTUI's grants, like those of the other institutes, helped fight the Cold War as well as providing services and support that many foreign unionists were seeking. In Poland, for instance, the institute not only helped Solidarity in its battle to organize an independent union. FTUI grants also bolstered those elements within the Polish trade union that were most dedicated to eradicating communist influence in the country and were most amenable to conservative economic and political strategies. By helping to keep the fires of protest lit in Poland, the U.S. federation also helped bring down the communist government.

As we discussed previously, FTUI's board of directors is drawn from the leadership of the AFL-CIO. Included are representatives from the labor federation's member unions, its international affairs department, and its regional affiliates. FTUI's executive director is Paul Somogyi, formerly the assistant director of the AFL-CIO's powerful department of international affairs. He succeeded Eugenia Kemble.

The American Institute for Free Labor Development (AIFLD), founded in 1962, is the international arm of the AFL-CIO in the western hemisphere and was the first of the four regional institutes to be established. Described by former CIA officer Philip Agee as a "CIA-controlled labor center financed through AID," AIFLD traces its origins to initiatives of the U.S. labor community and government in response to the Cuban revolution.[1] As explained in a staff report prepared for a congressional subcommittee in 1968, AIFLD was formed "primarily in response to the threat of Castroite infiltration and eventual control of major labor movements within Latin America."[2]

On the labor side, AIFLD was modeled on a training program for Latin American communications workers launched in the late 1950s by Joseph Beirne, president of the Communications Workers of America (CWA). Some 16 union leaders—members of unions affiliated with the Postal, Telegraph and Telephone Workers International—were brought to CWA's training center in Fort Royal, Virginia for a three-month course in "democratic unionism." The participants returned to their home countries following the training armed with a nine month stipend and the principles of "free" (i.e. conservative, probusiness, and anticommunist) trade unionism. Impressed favorably by the project, the AFL-CIO commissioned Beirne to plan a training institute for all Latin American unions and in May 1961 decided to create the organization he proposed.

In March of the same year, President John Kennedy had announced his plans to initiate the Alliance for Progress. An ambitious but ill-conceived program, the Alliance aimed at stifling Latin American radicalism through a two-pronged strategy. On the one hand, the Alliance was to promote regional economic development and social reforms in order to drain off popular support for radical change in the region. On the other hand, the Alliance was simultaneously to strengthen Latin American militaries so that they could crush popular challenges to the region's governments. Expanded U.S. government aid would be funneled through both governmental and non-governmental institutions, of which labor would be one. AIFLD became the AFL-CIO's conduit for U.S. government funds targeted for Alliance labor projects.

In a related initiative, Kennedy called for the creation of a Labor Advisory Committee on Foreign Policy, to be chaired by Secretary of Labor Arthur Goldberg. George Meany, then president of the AFL-CIO, was a member of the committee, and top-level representatives of the State Department and the CIA attended the sessions.[3] This committee arranged for $350,000 from U.S. government coffers to be used to set up AIFLD's first training program. Although the funds were to be used "to facilitate securing funding from private foundations, organizations, and companies," only a small number of private contributions were ever received.[4]

The presence of the CIA at meetings to discuss labor's role in U.S. foreign policy presaged AIFLD's involvement in the undercover operations of the U.S. government. AIFLD and its Latin American allies participated in CIA-backed destabilizations of democratically elected governments in various countries, including the Dominican Republic, Chile, and Guyana.[5] Similarly, in El Salvador during the early 1980s, AIFLD staff members Mark Pearlman and Michael Hammer—agrarian reform specialists gunned down with a Salvadoran counterpart—were identified by the U.S. solicitor-general as "some kind of undercover persons working under the cover of a labor organization."[6]

Over the years AIFLD has been active in almost every country in the western hemisphere. It uses U.S. government funds to sponsor education and training programs, provide technical assistance, conduct labor exchanges, support social service projects, and back the publication efforts of pro-U.S. unions. Assisting allied unions to develop political-action capacities has become a new focus of AIFLD and the other labor institutes. These projects include political education programs, voter registration, get-out-the-vote drives, media campaigns, election observation, trade union rights monitoring efforts, and visitor exchanges.

The African-American Labor Center (AALC), founded in 1964, is active in some 31 countries ranging from Angola to Zimbabwe. Its founder and first director was longtime labor activist and CIA operative Irving Brown.[7] He molded the institute into an anticommunist organization that spread the doctrine of labor-business harmony and bread-and-butter unionism to its African beneficiaries. Under Brown, the AALC became a vehicle for funneling U.S. aid to procapitalist, economistic African trade unions, a role which it continues to play today. When he met with South African unionists in 1973, for example, he warned them away from political activism against apartheid and urged them to concentrate on "practical" issues such as collective bargaining. He also offered technical and financial aid to unions with "responsible" Black leadership.[8]

The institute is still known in South Africa as an organization interested primarily in the "creation of a clearly capitalist society where labor is not so radical," says Kenneth Mokoena of the National Security Archive, a research institute based in Washington DC. According to Mokoena, whose research has concentrated on U.S. initiatives in South Africa, the AALC's trainings "emphasize probusiness unionism" and are more concerned with "working conditions, not general political relationships."[9]

The AALC builds and finances trade union education centers throughout the continent where it trains unionists through courses, seminars, and workshops. It also supports visitor exchanges, conducts development projects, and sponsors job-creation schemes. Recipients of its grants and training have promoted essentially harmonious relationships with management, tend to be politically quiescent, and, until recently, were known as collaborationists with South Africa's apartheid regime.

The activities of the American Institute for Free Labor Development—and, to a lesser extent, the Free Trade Union Institute—have stimulated controversy and a certain amount of scrutiny, but the operations of the AALC have been clouded in obscurity. Like the other institutes, however, the AALC has been accused of fronting for CIA operations in the region. Certainly the key role played by Irving Brown in the institute is a major factor supporting this conclusion.

One former intelligence officer, Paul Sakwa, identified Brown as a funnel for CIA cash to Kenya's Tom Mboya, a rightist politician backed by the United States until his murder in 1969.[10] Brown also helped organize the National Front for the Liberation of Angola, a CIA-sponsored rebel army headed by Holden Roberto. Brown's support for Roberto's "labor" activities was a cover for funneling cash to the group.[11] Another important figure whose activities with the AALC drew suspicion was Nelson "Nana" Mahomo. Mahomo—suspended and eventually expelled from the Pan-African Congress due to allegations of financial improprieties and cooperation with the CIA—was selected by the AALC in 1982 to head its Program of Action in Support of Black Trade Unions.[12] This selection occurred in spite of the fact that Mahomo had been absent from Africa for some 20 years and had had no experience as a trade unionist.

The political context surrounding labor activities in Africa contains significant factors which influence the AALC's operations on the continent. Africa's recent colonial past, its history of foreign intervention and domination, extremes of poverty and unemployment, and the importance of East/West divisions in national labor movements are some of these factors. Such factors led to deeply militant and nationalist labor movements, often allied with political parties and movements which pushed for decolonization. Following independence, however, many of these same militant labor organizations became junior partners to the new political elites.[13]

The U.S. federation was supportive of Africa's decolonization process—which perhaps not incidentally opened the door for U.S. involvement on the continent. While backing the withdrawal of the European powers, however, the AFL-CIO and later the AALC furthered U.S. entry into African affairs. They also paved the way for the acceptance of U.S. corporate expansion among indigenous labor movements. Their emphasis on bread-and-butter unionism and their predilection for institution-building over activism encouraged an already emerging trend in the region toward the deradicalization and bureaucratization of once-activist labor unions.[14] During the Cold War, U.S. labor projects amplified East/West divisions and undercut labor unity, stimulating competition among labor organizations both on ideological grounds and in pursuit of material support.[15]

Institute documents regarding Libya, for instance, counseled that "Libya is developing an increasing presence on the continent as an agent of subversion." In response, according to the documents, "AALC programs seek to offset...these [Libyan and other continent-wide subversive movements] through a combination of institution-building, exchanges, organizational cooperation, and other efforts."[16] In Chad—a target of a Libyan-backed rebel movement—the African institute countered Libya's actions by supporting the government-linked

Workers Confederation of Chad. Chad's Unatrat union federation, however, was described by the AALC as "Libyan-supported" and thus missed out on institute backing even though more moderate elements of the AALC wanted to strengthen ties with the federation.[17]

More than any of the AFL-CIO's other international institutes, the AALC cooperates with regional labor organizations and supports them with funding, technical assistance, and other services. Among its beneficiaries are the Organization of African Trade Union Unity (OATUU), a pan-African association of trade unions. The AALC also supports regional institutions such as the Southern African Trade Union Coordinating Council (SATUCC), the Organization of Trade Unions of West Africa (OTUWA), and the Organization of Central African Workers (OTAC). In addition to these strictly African entities, the institute provides support to and through the African Regional Organization of the International Confederation of Free Trade Unions.

The Asian-American Free Labor Institute (AAFLI) was founded by the AFL-CIO executive council in 1968 to operate as labor's arm in Vietnam. Shortly thereafter, AAFLI expanded its operations to include the Philippines and other Asian and Pacific countries. It now supports unions in approximately 30 countries in Asia, the Pacific, and the Middle East, with resident representatives in Bangladesh, Indonesia, South Korea, the Philippines, Thailand, and Turkey.

Like AIFLD, the Asian institute was launched in response to the Cold War factors in the international arena. The AFL-CIO's growing dissatisfaction with the ICFTU because of the socialist and social-democratic orientations of some of its members was one such factor. The opposition of many ICFTU member unions to the U.S. war in Vietnam was another. Creation of an institution such as AAFLI increasingly was seen as necessary in order to provide an alternative vehicle for AFL-CIO bilateral interactions with Asian unionists.

Another incident that impelled AAFLI's founding was the Tet offensive in Vietnam. According to AAFLI documents, the institute was set up to help distribute relief supplies, some of them funneled through CARE, after the flogging U.S. allies took during the offensive. Soon thereafter the institute began conducting trainings and other projects. Its beneficiary in the country was Tran Quoc Buu, the corrupt but anticommunist leader of the Vietnamese Confederation of Labor (CVT). Reminiscent of union efforts in postwar Europe, the CVT—allied with the U.S.-backed regime of Nguyen Van Thieu—supported CIA and U.S. military efforts by keeping the docks open to permit entry of vital supplies. In outlying areas, CVT unionists cooperated with U.S.-sponsored pacification campaigns.

Like the other institutes, AAFLI has been accused of providing cover for U.S. intelligence operations. In fact, former CIA operative Philip Agee charged that AAFLI is permeated with "principal CIA agents."[18] Agee identified Morris Paladino—former deputy executive director of AIFLD, former executive director of AAFLI, and former AFL-CIO official with the International Confederation of Free Trade Unions—as the "principal CIA agent for control of the [Interamerican Regional Organization of Workers]," the ICFTU's regional arm for Latin America.[19] In addition, the institute's first secretary-treasurer, James Suffridge, came from the Retail Clerks International Association, a U.S. union through which the CIA ran operations with white-collar workers.[20] Suffridge had suggested that union-to-union programs in Asia be funded as far back as 1961 but AID and the AFL-CIO were at that time concentrating on getting the Latin American institute off the ground.[21] Valentine Suazo, another AAFLI representative with a background in AIFLD's Latin American labor activities, has also been alleged to have CIA links.[22]

Foreign intervention and domination—expressed through past colonial and current neocolonial relationships—have helped to shape Asian trade unionism. As Dave Spooner, an analyst at the Asia Monitor Resource Center put it, "The union structures, practices and labour laws of countries such as South Korea, Taiwan, the Philippines, Malaysia, India and elsewhere, are as much the result of support, imposition or manipulation by the governments, political parties and trade unions of Europe and the U.S., as they are of the activities of workers themselves."[23] One outcome of this historical reality is a frequent emphasis by more militant unions on nationalism, anti-imperialism, and national liberation as components of "genuine" trade unionism.[24]

Most national labor movements in Asia are characterized by cleavages along ideological, religious, or ethnic lines which result in the formation of rival national union centers. The Philippines, for example, has given rise to four such centers, two of which—the Trade Union Congress of the Philippines and the Kilusang Mayo Uno, or May First Movement—are in vigorous competition for the loyalties of workers.

Close ties to national political parties and other elements of national ruling structures is another common feature of Asian trade unionism. The Fiji Trades Union Congress—supported by AAFLI—launched the Fiji Labor Party in 1985 and has often been closely aligned with the Fijian government. Likewise, the AAFLI-backed Federation of Korean Trade Unions in South Korea, the Trade Union Congress of the Philippines, and the All-Indonesia Workers' Union (SPSI) each have close relations with the military, business community, and/or government in their respective countries.[25]

The dangers of such alliances for independent and principled trade unionism are obvious. They also contradict the AFL-CIO's oft-repeated claim that it backs "free" trade unions around the world. Ernesto Herrera, the general secretary of the Philippine federation and a member of Corazón Aquino's slate in the national Senate, inadvertently demonstrated the dangers while calling for tighter labor laws in the country. Labor leaders "who do not adhere to the national agenda of industrial peace," he said, "[must] be arrested."[26]

In addition to its connections with national labor bodies, AAFLI is linked to the ICFTU's regional arm in Asia and the Pacific, the Asia-Pacific Regional Organization (APRO). Based in Singapore, the Asia-Pacific organization coordinates the activities of ICFTU affiliates in the area.

Multinational Labor Organizations

Along with the regional institutes, the AFL-CIO's membership in international labor organizations provides an important avenue for influencing labor trends and political affairs overseas. For example, the federation and its institutes are represented in the International Confederation of Free Trade Unions (ICFTU) and the International Labor Organization. By participating in such bodies, the federation advances a variety of important labor causes. It has, for example, supported the development of international conventions on labor designed to safeguard basic rights of union organizing and set standards on workplace health and safety. But these memberships also enhance the AFL-CIO's capacity to shape international labor legislation, disseminate its conservative analysis of labor's role in a capitalist system, and ostracize and delegitimize militant unions.

As a member of the Brussels-based ICFTU, for instance, the U.S. federation has ties to a range of union confederations with national and international influence, which can act as advocates for and allies of the U.S. labor federation's favored policies. But the ICFTU is important to the United States not only as an avenue for interaction with labor' sectors around the world. As the largest and most influential non-communist international labor federation, it also holds consultative status in the United Nations, International Labor Organization, and other international bodies. Its affiliation with the ICFTU offers the AFL-CIO a multilateral pulpit from which to address these intergovernmental bodies and press for its desired policies. In the International Labor Organization, for example, the ICFTU helps coordinate the activities of the worker delegations to the ILO Conference, its committees, and governing body.

The British Trades Union Congress, along with the American Federation of Labor and the Congress of Industrial Organizations, engineered the creation of the ICFTU in 1949 as a breakaway from the socialist-led World Federation of Trade Unions. Today the international confederation includes diverse national union centers including conservative, social-democratic, and socialist perspectives. The ICFTU's major unions hail from West Germany, Britain, the United States, Scandinavia, and Japan. Recently, with the downfall of the Soviet bloc in Eastern Europe, the confederation has established contacts with anticommunist unions in Czechoslovakia, Romania, Bulgaria, and Poland.[27] Even with this range of unions, however, the ICFTU still holds philosophically to a reformist vision of international labor relations. In general, its activities are designed to maintain traditional capitalist relationships and to minimize tensions between labor and business.

The AFL-CIO has had a love-hate relationship with the confederation since shortly after its founding. The influence of socialist unions within the organization and the opposition of European unions to the U.S. war in Vietnam even led the AFL-CIO to leave the confederation in the late 1960s. In 1982, the AFL-CIO reaffiliated with the international federation, but the U.S. federation's major field activities continue to be sponsored through its own institutes or through the international trade secretariats associated with the ICFTU.

The international confederation's Latin American affiliate, the Interamerican Regional Organization of Workers (ORIT), was established as a result of the efforts of the AFL's Serafino Romualdi. Its African arm is the African Regional Organization, and in Asia, the Asia-Pacific Regional Organization acts as its regional affiliate.

Another important international forum for the AFL-CIO is the International Labor Organization (ILO). The ILO is a tripartite body which incorporates government, employers, and union leaders. An outgrowth of the League of Nations, the ILO was established in 1919 with the assistance of the AFL's Samuel Gompers. As president of the Commission on Labor Legislation of the Versailles Peace Conference, Gompers drafted the documents outlining the tripartite structure of the organization.[28] The organization responded to concerns in the major capitalist powers that overexploitation of labor was contributing to social unrest and possible revolutionary sentiments in industrialized countries.[29] Fears that the Russian revolution would stimulate similar movements elsewhere led governments and business leaders in the West to accept the reformist labor legislation and standards pressed by procapitalist union federations like the AFL-CIO. The ILO was set up to monitor working conditions and raise the living standards of workers worldwide, all within the general framework of global capitalism.

The three major international confederations, the ICFTU, World Federation of Trade Unions, and World Confederation of Labor, each hold full consultative status with the ILO. In turn, the ILO since 1946 has had a formal relationship with the United Nations.

Even with the participation of the communist unions of the World Federation of Trade Unions, the ILO promotes the notion that governments and business can be brought into a mutually beneficial social pact with labor. Rejecting the notion that labor and employers are natural class enemies, the ILO—like the U.S. labor federation—believes that economic and social development result from the cooperation of workers, government, and business.

Although the ILO has no power to enforce its recommended standards on labor, it plays an important role in setting norms about treatment of workers around the world. Its conventions and recommendations—on issues ranging from human rights to social security—come into force when they are ratified by member governments. If governments or employers fail to uphold those conventions, complaints may be brought against them before the appropriate ILO committees and conferences. Like other multinational bodies, however, the ILO's censure may or may not be persuasive. Its effectiveness depends on a government's sensitivity to criticism on labor issues and whether that criticism can be turned into more substantive forms of pressure such as exclusion from favored trade status with other member governments of the ILO.

The ILO represents a significant forum for the AFL-CIO's efforts to influence international unionism. It is not, however, one which the U.S. federation can control. A case in point occurred following the CIA-backed coup which overthrew the democratically elected government of Salvador Allende in Chile. The AFL-CIO and AIFLD supported the Chilean National Workers' Confederation, known as an apologist for the savage and labor-repressive Chilean junta. The ILO refused to grant accreditation to the Chilean confederation despite the prodding of the U.S. labor federation.[30] In a similar vein, the AFL-CIO delegation walked out of the 1975 conference of the international organization to protest the decision of the ILO to grant observer status to the Palestine Liberation Organization.

In 1977 the United States withdrew temporarily from the organization, citing what it felt was growing communist influence. Prior to the rift, Carl Gershman argued that the "trouble" in the ILO began in 1954 when unions with communist affiliations were admitted. "The growing weight of Third World nations in the ILO in the early 1960s,"

Gershman wrote, "eroded American influence as it enhanced Russia's ability to form anti-American alliances."[31]

The AFL-CIO also participates in the Trade Union Advisory Committee (TUAC) of the Organization for Economic Cooperation and Development (OECD). Even more than the other international bodies on which the AFL-CIO is represented, the OECD speaks directly for the developed countries of North America, Western Europe, and Japan. It grew out of U.S. efforts to rebuild Western Europe after World War II and is designed to encourage economic cooperation between industrialized capitalist nations. The ubiquitous Irving Brown was instrumental in founding the advisory committee, which was formally organized in 1948. The committee presses labor issues before the OECD, focusing on those issues important both to developed countries and the third world.

As with the International Labor Organization and the ICFTU, the U.S. labor federation's attempts to shape international unionism are sometimes fettered by the TUAC's multinational members. For instance, the advisory committee accepted the affiliation of the Italian General Confederation of Labor (CGIL) over the objections of the AFL-CIO. The U.S. federation argued that the CGIL was dominated by communists and thus should not be accepted into the labor committee. It was joined in its objections by four union confederations in Japan, France, and Portugal.[32] Of the four confederations, at least two of them, the Force Ouvrière (Workers Force) in France and the General Union of Workers in Portugal, have long been major beneficiaries of the AFL-CIO.

Other Labor Internationals

The International Confederation of Free Trade Unions competes for the affiliations of the world's trade unionists with two other international confederations, one communist and one with Christian roots. The World Federation of Trade Unions (WFTU) was founded in 1945 by the CIO and trade unions from Britain, France, and the Soviet Union. The AFL refused to join because of the involvement of Soviet trade unions. By 1949, as Cold War tensions heightened and in response to the WFTU's rejection of the Marshall Plan, the CIO and European unions split from the federation. Since that time, the federation has linked unions from the communist world with various non-aligned unions in the third world. The disintegration of the Soviet bloc has seriously damaged the federation, although, as of the early 1990s, it is still sponsoring meetings, producing publications, and supporting unions in third world countries.

The WFTU's regional organization in Latin America is the Permanent Congress of Unified Trade Unions of Latin American Workers

(CPUSTAL). No particular organizations within the WFTU specifically cover Africa or Asia, although the federation does have union affiliates in places like the Philippines. International associations of trade unions called Trade Unions International (TUI) are also linked to the WFTU. The TUI are similar to the international trade secretariats of the ICFTU.

Progressive critics of the WFTU have faulted it on grounds remarkably similar to charges directed against the AFL-CIO: restricted levels of internal democracy, "political subservience" to a superpower (in this case, the Soviet Union), and use of an East/West prism to view issues of third world unionism.[33] One marxist critic blasted the WFTU for its "doctrinaire Marxism" which, he charged, prevented the WFTU from developing a clear analysis of the "complex structure of the working class and labouring poor in the Third World" and inspired a "rigid conception of the transition to socialism in the Third World."[34]

Historically the AFL-CIO has maintained a hard-line "shunning" position in opposition to contact with the WFTU or its affiliated unions. "Contact with such organizations does not advance the interests of peace or human rights," the AFL-CIO has declared. "[I]t only confers legitimacy on anti-democratic and anti-worker institutions and harms the courageous democratic activists jailed and murdered by Communist rulers."[35]

The World Confederation of Labor (WCL) is the smallest and oldest of the three international labor confederations. Its roots can be traced back to 1920 when European trade unions formed the International Confederation of Christian Trade Unionists. The organization adopted its current name in 1968. Although it no longer emphasizes its Roman Catholic heritage, the WCL still blends Christian-socialist beliefs with anticommunism and a non-aligned position regarding the ICFTU and WFTU.

Like the other international confederations, the WCL has been active in the third world. It has two regional affiliates, the Latin American Confederation of Workers (CLAT) and the Brotherhood of Asian Trade Unionists (BATU). These affiliates, like the WCL itself, have a "more nuanced appreciation" of class issues in the third world than either the ICFTU or the WFTU, according to some observers.[36] In Latin America, for example, CLAT advocates nationalist and social justice positions which often pit it against AIFLD. In practice, however, it also has supported Christian Democrat governments—as in Venezuela—despite conservative policies which are often harmful to labor.

**Table 2: Working Through the International Trade Secretariats:
The AFL-CIO and Union-to-Union Programs**
(selected examples)

U.S. Union	International Trade Secretariat	U.S. Govt. Funding Agency	Years	Program
American Federation of Teachers	International Federation of Free Teachers Unions	AID	1989	week-long seminar focusing on union administration, union functions, and grievance handling for leaders of the Union of Protestant Teachers of Togo
American Federation of Teachers (AFT)	International Federation of Free Teachers Unions	NED	1987-88	for a program coordinated by the AFT's International Affairs Department to study "Teachers Under Dictatorship," focusing on South Africa, Poland, Chile, and Nicaragua
Communications Workers of America	Postal, Telegraph, and Telephone International	NED	1985	organizing and educational activities

International Association of Machinists and Aerospace Workers	International Metal Workers Federation	AID	1987-89	regional seminar for union staff on personal computers; purchase of personal computers for ten unions in various Asian countries
International Union of Bricklayers and Allied Craftsmen (IUBAC)	International Federation of Building and Woodworkers	AID	1988	IUBAC President John Joyce and his international affairs adviser, Joel Freedman, along with AALC deputy director David Brombart traveled to Tunisia, Mali, Zimbabwe, Mozambique, and Egypt, offering cooperation

Sources: African-American Labor Center, *1988 Annual Report on Grant. No. AFR-0441-A-00-5017-00*, submitted to AID, March 31, 1989; African-American Labor Center, *1989 Annual Report on Grant No. AFR-0441-A-00-5017-00*, submitted to AID, March 1990; Grant No. ANE-0263-G-SS-7028-04, Amendment No. 4, between AAFLI and AID, April 1, 1989; Quarterly activity and financial report, submitted by FTUI to NED, January 31, 1988; Proposal from FTUI to NED, November 18, 1985; and "Free Trade Union Institute Status Report on Active FY84 and FY85 Programs," prepared for the Board of Directors of the National Endowment for Democracy, June 3, 1986.

International Trade Secretariats

Among the most significant vehicles for AFL-CIO support to foreign unions are the international trade secretariats (ITS). Associated with the ICFTU, but technically independent of it, the ITS are international bodies which link unionists in the same industries in different countries. Generally more flexible and responsive than the international confederations, the secretariats focus more on issues of daily importance to their affiliates and less on governmental relationships and representation in intergovernmental bodies.[37]

On an international level, the ITS receive the majority of their funding from their primary affiliates in the United States, Europe, and Japan. Funding for the AFL-CIO's programs through the ITS, however, generally originates in the U.S. government. Funneled first through the Agency for International Development or the National Endowment for Democracy, the AFL-CIO distributes subgrants either through its labor institutes or directly to AFL-CIO unions affiliated with a given secretariat. The grants pay for international exchanges, conferences, civic education and political activities, technical assistance, union-building, equipment and vehicles, office support, and program design.

Although the AFL-CIO has supported union-to-union projects through a wide variety of trade secretariats, it has worked extensively with unions in such strategic sectors as transportation, telecommunications, the postal service, government employees, and other public services. Unions like these are particularly influential during sensitive political and economic events, such as strikes and coups. Certain U.S. unions involved in these programs—such as the Retail Clerks International Association—and secretariats such as the Postal, Telegraph, and Telephone International and the International Federation of Petroleum and Chemical Workers have been used to run CIA operations.

Affiliations to the international trade secretariats of the ICFTU provide access to resources, legitimacy, and a certain amount of protection from repression. Because of their monetary contributions, the AFL-CIO and its institutes carry substantial weight in most of the trade secretariats. Thus, when it comes time to make decisions about which unions to affiliate to a given ITS, the U.S. federation has considerable influence over the outcome. But that influence does not always translate into AFL-CIO dominance. In El Salvador, for example, a long-running battle to affiliate the Coffee Industry Union (SICAFE) to the International Union of Food and Allied Workers' Associations (IUF) was fought tooth and nail by the AFL-CIO, which had labeled the Salvadoran union as communist. The IUF's 1990 decision to affiliate the Salvadoran coffeeworkers union over the objections of

AIFLD and the AFL-CIO pulled the rug out from under the U.S. labor federation's attempt to smear the union as "undemocratic" and a tool of the Salvadoran guerrillas.

Ironically, working within multinational labor organizations like the ITS helps to shield the U.S. federation's activities from public view even though the AFL-CIO may be working right alongside other labor organizations that do not share its beliefs or that advocate different strategies. As with other federation activities, it is a time-consuming and complicated task to trace the funds and analyze the consequences of the AFL-CIO's involvement in these multilateral organizations. Holding the federation accountable in these activities is a formidable undertaking that requires the interest and efforts not only of the U.S. public and Congress, but of unionists overseas. Such coordinated action is even more crucial because of the magnitude of the federation's operations in other countries and their often harmful consequences for foreign labor.

CHAPTER FOUR
Institute Programs and Activities

Projects carried out by the AFL-CIO's own institutes or through the international trade secretariats are the primary mechanisms by which the AFL-CIO gains influence in foreign labor sectors. The institutes sponsor projects in several main categories of activities. These include education and training, agrarian union development, social projects, information dissemination and visitor exchanges, and political action. Institution-building is another major activity of the labor institutes and is designed to strengthen national labor federations and individual unions whose interests and methods run parallel to U.S. foreign policy needs. The U.S.-funded labor projects create patronage networks which enhance the appeal of allied unions and school up-and-coming union leaders in the principles and tactics of "business" and "bread-and-butter" unionism. In addition, recent emphasis on directly political activities such as voter registration and get-out-the-vote drives has magnified the political impact of the institutes, as they directly fund and guide programs aimed at selecting political leaders overseas.

Educating "Free" Trade Unions

The institutes' education activities include trainings at the local, national, regional, and international levels, aimed at the rank and file as well as union leaders. Because of the AFL-CIO's emphasis on the shop-floor aspects of unionism, course content stresses nuts-and-bolts labor topics such as techniques of collective bargaining, organization and administration of "free" trade unions, methods of conducting labor research, and conflict resolution. But the anticommunist fervor of the labor federation is represented too, in overtly political courses on political ideologies ("democracy" versus "totalitarianism") and international economics.[1]

71

The courses offered in AFL-CIO trainings have political payoffs for the United States. In addition to defusing the militancy of foreign labor, the classes transmit a generally positive view of U.S. foreign policy and the U.S. political and economic system. Moreover, courses offered by the labor institutes help the AFL-CIO gain entry into foreign unions and shape their attitudes toward politics, economics, and the role of trade unions in society. The courses are used to identify prospective leaders of national union movements who are then sent on for further U.S.-sponsored trainings, thus embedding them in the AFL-CIO's worldview. These leaders are often returned to their national union centers as "interns," with stipends paid by the AFL-CIO. On various occasions, these trainees have acted as partners in activities with serious political repercussions. In Chile during the coup in 1973, for example, AIFLD-trained communications and maritime workers kept lines open for the military.[2]

In South Africa, the African labor institute is trying to create a cadre of "Western-influenced labor leaders that can be brought to the United States to promote the views [on South Africa] that the conservatives in the AFL-CIO hold to," says Kenneth Mokoena of the National Security Archive. The AALC's trainings, Mokoena contends, are aimed at developing union leaders "who emphasize working conditions, not politics, who promote business, who don't promote nationalization, and who definitely don't emphasize labor dominance over business." The AALC "clearly has a political agenda, a particular purpose in South Africa," Mokoena insists. Its trainings are just one means by which the labor institute hopes to "gain influence in the post-apartheid system and to promote U.S. foreign policy interests."[3]

The programs offered by the AFL-CIO today represent an abrupt shift from U.S. labor education in the early twentieth century. As noted by one critic, labor education was originally "a radical cultural and political enterprise. Its goals transcended teaching union skills, and focused on arousing working class consciousness, identifying working class culture, and developing commitments to progressive socio-economic and political change."[4] By the advent of the Cold War, U.S. labor's educational programs had become "trivialized," in the words of Stanley Aronowitz, and focused on "supporting and enlarging the influence of the trade union bureaucracies."[5]

Each of the institutes is deeply involved in conducting education and training activities and there seems to be little difference in the major types of programs offered in different regions. At the local level, however, coursework is often targeted to the specific needs of unions in given countries. In Zimbabwe, for example, the African institute's 1988 trainings included an analysis of the country's national security policy. Similarly, in 1989, the Asian institute offered training in Employee Stock Ownership Plans to union leaders, state enterprise managers, and government policy makers in Thailand.

AIFLD's trainings provide a good example of the extent of the AFL-CIO's educational projects. Classes are offered in-country, regionally at institutes such as the AIFLD-backed Central American Institute for Labor Studies (IESCA) in Honduras, and in the United States at the George Meany Center for Labor Studies. From 1962 to 1989, some 650,000 unionists participated in in-country programs, and some went on to regional classes or to the United States for intensive trainings.[6] Such activities are designed to have a multiplier effect, with U.S.-trained unionists teaching their local counterparts and U.S. influence gradually rippling out through foreign labor movements. Like AIFLD, the African institute emphasizes education and has established labor education centers in Ghana, Egypt, Kenya, Lesotho, Mauritius, and Zaire. In Asia, AAFLI's education seminars by 1985 had trained more than 227,000 unionists. In 1988 alone it conducted 1,450 training programs with more than 56,000 participants.[7]

Education offered by the AFL-CIO's institutes provides foreign unionists with opportunities unlikely in their home countries, thus reinforcing their patronage appeal. One example is the Asian institute's Participant Training Program, which offers instruction in administrative and technical skills. According to AAFLI, the training program is "an integral part of its trade union development in the Middle East, South Pacific, and Asia."[8] Grants pay for tuition, travel, living expenses, supplies, and equipment for unionists and officials of foreign labor ministries to attend trainings in the United States or third world countries. Participants typically attend classes at the Harvard University Trade Union Program, the University of Wisconsin Center for Cooperatives, and the U.S. Bureau of Labor Statistics International Labor Statistics Program Center. One of the other countries that has hosted these grant recipients is Israel, at its International Institute for Development, Cooperation and Labor Studies in Tel Aviv.

Seminars on the "Role of Unions in a Democratic Society," "Recognition and Analysis of Extremist Propaganda," and courses which indoctrinate workers about "communist strategies" for infiltrating and taking power in unions have been held in countries ranging from Nicaragua to South Korea. In Grenada, for example, AIFLD conducted a seminar on political theories and systems immediately following the U.S. invasion. The program responded to U.S. government interest in developing the "democratic" union organizations in the country and involved the participation of the Seaman's and Waterfront Workers' Union (SWWU), along with four other unions.

The SWWU had collaborated with U.S. troops during the invasion and later volunteered time to erase revolutionary slogans from buildings and walls.[9]

In Guatemala, where the Latin American institute supports the Confederation of Guatemalan Trade Union Unity (CUSG), U.S. assistance has been very important for the group's educational programs. Antonio Alfaro, the director of the confederation's center for education and organization, says that "It would be almost impossible to do our work without AIFLD's financial help." CUSG officials are trained at the AFL-CIO's George Meany Center where they attend seminars on topics such as "comparative economic systems" and "democracy and development."

CUSG activist Juan de Dios Herrera described the importance of AIFLD trainings and incidentally revealed some of the indoctrination that is woven into the coursework. "The George Meany Center plays a very important role throughout Latin America," Herrera explained. "Without it we wouldn't know all of the problems of Latin America. They taught us advanced techniques of unionism, economics, the political economy of the United States, pluralism in the U.S., and about the United Nations," he continued. "Thanks to you guys," Herrera concluded, "I learned what a democratic union is."[10]

Institute education programs are also used to bolster allies overseas and to attract new workers to the U.S.-backed unions. In South Korea, AAFLI's trainings for the Federation of Korean Trade Unions (FKTU) skyrocketed after the formation there of a militant, broad-based coalition of independent trade unions in January 1990.[11] The challenge to the FKTU—which has historical ties to the South Korean government and is the only legal union center in the country—was mounted by the *Chun-no-hyup* federation, known in English as the Korea Trade Union Congress. Politically, the new trade union congress aims "to resist and defeat the capitalist and state powers responsible for labour movement repression."[12] It also presses for increased wage levels, reduction of the work week to 44 hours, and various other economistic demands. In contrast, the U.S.-backed federation frequently has moderated its wage requests in response to government pressures and has been encouraged by AAFLI to "stick to the straight and narrow economic issues."[13]

But sticking to the "straight and narrow economic issues" often saps unions of much-needed militancy. A Honduran unionist who took part in AIFLD trainings said that the classes were designed to produce docile and conservative labor leaders. "AIFLD," she charged, "wants to make labor leaders play the role of plugs, as stoppers which block the advancement of the labor movement."

Enrolling Peasants in the Pro-U.S. Coalition

Agricultural workers in the third world are a high-priority target for the AFL-CIO's projects overseas. Frequently unorganized, agrarian workers generally constitute the largest workforce in underdeveloped countries. Whether small farmers or landless laborers, these workers are strategic populations in economies that rely on the agricultural sector for foreign exchange earnings and for basic foodstuffs for urban populations. Their cooperation is also very important for economic strategies that seek export-led solutions to debt problems. Rising militancy among this population, the strategic value of the agrarian sector, the perception that small farmers could be mobilized as small capitalists, and the simple fact that so many workers still labor in rural areas led the AFL-CIO institutes to concentrate programs on this sector. Among the countries targeted for the AFL-CIO's agrarian projects are El Salvador, the Dominican Republic, Venezuela, Bangladesh, Indonesia, Sri Lanka, and Mauritius.

The agrarian programs sponsored by the institutes often provide important benefits and services to rural workers overseas. They also, however, help to pacify populations who might otherwise join revolutionary movements in a frustrated effort to press their governments and their employers to provide needed services, redistribute landholdings, and raise wages to livable levels. In addition, they drain off supporters from organizations which pursue broad programs of social and political reforms and help counter the appeal of leftist movements.

The Honduran National Association of Agricultural Workers (ANACH) was created in the early 1960s with the support of the American Institute for Free Labor Development. ANACH was intended as a counterweight to the strong organizing among campesinos by groups associated with the communist party. After linking up with other AIFLD-backed unions in the country, the agricultural workers federation maintained a friendly relationship with military governments during the 1960s and 1970s. Its ties to the Latin American institute were strengthened over the years, not only with financial support, but with AIFLD backing for service projects such as housing for agricultural workers.

Until recently, ANACH took a conservative approach to Honduran rural affairs. The association pushed for the enforcement of the agrarian reform law by working through political parties and attempting to reach an accord with the government. As one ANACH representative explained, "We are of a social democratic tendency, and we go through the National Agrarian Institute to get land for our members."[14] Unfortunately, however, the Honduran government's land reform institute rarely distributes land without pressure. In recognition of this reality, the association has become increasingly militant and has joined coalitions with other more progressive labor and campesino organizations. In the process ANACH has distanced itself from the strategies promoted by its U.S. sponsor.

A peasant from a rival federation described AIFLD's general approach in Honduras, "More than anything else, AIFLD promotes a political strategy that says there should be cooperation between the worker and the boss. We believe, however, and have found it to be true, that only through pressure and through struggle does the boss give concessions to the workers."[15]

The most developed of the U.S. federation's agrarian programs is AIFLD's Agrarian Union Development Service, later renamed the Agrarian Union Development Department (AUDD). Launched in 1965, the AUDD has assisted allied peasant unions and associations in organizing, training their leaders, establishing production and marketing cooperatives, and sponsoring community development projects in areas such as literacy and sanitation. It also has supported land titling and agrarian reform programs. A major emphasis of the AUDD during the 1980s has been the linking of rural and urban unions into national movements capable of mounting joint political and economic actions in their countries.[16] Among the countries served by such programs during the 1980s have been El Salvador, Honduras, Bolivia, Ecuador, and the Dominican Republic. Another AUDD union beneficiary is the Confederation of Guatemalan Trade Union Unity (CUSG), a center-right social democratic union founded under the Ríos Montt dictatorship in 1983 in part to qualify Guatemala for participation in the Caribbean Basin Initiative.

In Nicaragua, a campesino program targeted rural affiliates of the U.S.-backed Confederation of Trade Union Unity (CUS) during the late 1980s. Participating cooperatives used NED funds to purchase seed, fertilizer, and insecticide. A portion of the costs of land rental and warehousing facilities was also covered by the grants. According to NED's 1985 annual report, the Nicaraguan union federation was "resisting [Sandinista] government control and repression," but the actual character of the union is more complicated than that. Organized in 1962, CUS was active in many businesses owned by the Somoza family dictatorship, including airlines and hotels, as well as certain agricultural enterprises. Known as a pro-government union under the Somozas, CUS turned aggressively anti-government with the rise to power of Nicaragua's leftist Sandinistas. Although a longtime beneficiary of AIFLD support, the Nicaraguan union's funding leaped dramatically after the Sandinista government was installed in 1979.[17] A 1985 report by a delegation of U.S. labor lawyers to Nicaragua found that the leadership and many members of the two Nicaraguan trade unions supported by the AFL-CIO [including CUS] were "politically aligned with forces seeking the violent overthrow of the Nicaraguan government."[18]

The Asian institute has a variety of programs focusing on the agrarian sector, including support for tea workers in Sri Lanka and plantation workers in West Java, Indonesia. The Ceylon Workers Congress used AAFLI funds for development projects with Indian Tamils working on tea estates in Sri Lanka. For instance, AAFLI provided a loan to purchase seeds, fertilizers, and insecticides for cooperative vegetable gardens on the estates. A medical training program for volunteer "barefoot doctors" was implemented and sanitation committees to clean up the tea worker communities were also created. In Indonesia, the All-Indonesia Workers' Union—the only federation approved by the government—supports plantation workers in West Java in community development projects. Bathing, washing, and latrine facilities were built with AAFLI support, and workers received assistance for the union's cooperative and home garden projects.

On the surface, projects like these are unobjectionable. They clearly provide many important services for their beneficiaries. Such services should, however, be provided through a living wage and a socioeconomic system that distributes the society's resources more equitably. By donating these necessities through U.S. labor programs, the AFL-CIO's institutes, whether intentionally or inadvertently, help to maintain an exploitable agrarian population that might otherwise mobilize to demand equity.

The labor institutes have also participated in land reform schemes explicitly designed to defuse rural militancy. In El Salvador, AIFLD designed the country's misconceived and poorly implemented 1980 land reform, under a contract with the Agency for International Development. To carry out the program, AIFLD hired Roy Prosterman, a professor at the University of Washington. Although he was unfamiliar with Latin America, Prosterman had other credentials which apparently appealed to AIFLD. He had worked in U.S.-sponsored agrarian counterinsurgency projects in Vietnam during the U.S. war there and was familiar with using agrarian reform as part of a package of political instruments designed to win support for U.S.-backed governments. His assistant in El Salvador was Cleto Di Giovanni, a former senior CIA officer with extensive experience in Latin America.[19] Like Prosterman, Di Giovanni had also served in Vietnam.[20]

Although partially successful, the agrarian reform in El Salvador did not provide land to the landless and was blocked repeatedly by entrenched elites in the country. Critics called it "just another U.S.

pacification program aimed at forcing some North American version of progress upon the Salvadorean people."[21] A delegation of U.S. unionists found that, without trade union freedom in El Salvador and given the structure of the land reform program, it was "difficult to see how the reform...could ever significantly impact on El Salvador's campesinos." The delegation concluded by questioning whether official U.S. efforts were likely to lead to enhancement of worker rights and living conditions, reporting that "The U.S. goal as explained by the Embassy was to give private investors confidence."[22]

Despite these failures and criticisms, Prosterman was hired by the U.S. State Department in the mid-1980s and sent to support the land reform of President Aquino in the Philippines. Prosterman, who had worked on the ineffectual agrarian reform programs of Ferdinand Marcos during the 1970s, said that his goals in the Philippines under the Aquino government were to diffuse peasant unrest and to use the land reform as an instrument of counterinsurgency.[23] During the 1980s, his office was in the AAFLI headquarters in Manila.

Winning Hearts Through Social Projects

The labor institutes fund various types of "membership services" which have nothing to do with labor-management relations but serve a variety of other important functions. According to the labor institutes, these other functions include: maintaining contact with constituencies when unions are under pressure from government, countering the effects of modernization of production, and maintaining a popular image for allied labor organizations when progress in wages and benefits is impossible. Social service projects also are powerful magnets to attract new members to unions supported by the AFL-CIO. As the African institute described it, service projects "have enabled union federations not only to improve members' standard of living but also to attract unorganized workers to the labor movement."

An assortment of programs are funded by grants and loans from the institutes. Child care facilities have been set up with the Thai Blanket Workers Union and the Luckytex Textile Workers Union in Thailand. Family planning services are offered to women in Bangladesh. Literacy programs operate in Zimbabwe and Botswana; credit unions and workplace savings societies have been set up in various countries, including Kenya and the Philippines. Likewise, medical and dental services funded by the labor institutes assist workers in places like Indonesia, Poland, Nicaragua, Ghana, and Zaire. Other social projects supported by the labor institutes have included worker housing construction and administration of project financing mechanisms such as the AID-funded Regional Revolving Loan Fund and the Caribbean Basin Labor Fund.

Membership services are designed to bolster unions friendly to the United States and to visibly transmit the notion that workers benefit under capitalist systems. The Caribbean Basin Labor Fund, for instance, instituted in 1983, has supported projects falling under the rubric of the Caribbean Basin Initiative. One of these projects involved sending tools to anti-Sandinista unionists in Nicaragua in 1988. The Trade Union Congress of the Philippines (TUCP) likewise received assistance for various projects both through the Agency for International Development and the National Endowment for Democracy. Don Phillips, AAFLI's representative in the Philippines, spoke of handing out NED money to Filipino families and acknowledged that the grants helped increase the TUCP's appeal in the country. "Imagine if you have $100,000 to give out to families in $500 chunks," Phillips told the *San Francisco Examiner.* "Your stock goes way up, faster than the stock of any of the militant groups."[24] According to the Asian institute in 1989, programs such as these helped the TUCP boost its membership by some 80,000 unionists and triple its income.[25]

As in the Philippines, membership services help to pacify populations who might otherwise organize against U.S.-backed governments. In El Salvador, following a 1989 offensive by the guerrillas of the Farabundo Marti National Liberation Front (FMLN), the AIFLD-supported National Union of Workers and Campesinos (UNOC) stepped in to provide services for members affected by the fighting. The labor institute assisted UNOC in gathering and distributing bags of food with provisions to last a family of five for a week. AIFLD also provided funds to purchase construction materials to repair members' houses, and unions affiliated to UNOC cleared away rubble and broken glass from areas suffering damage.

During the late 1980s, the African institute concentrated heavily on job creation and income-generating activities sponsored by AALC-backed unions. These projects have multiple purposes, including raising revenue for the unions themselves, providing social welfare benefits for union members, and attracting new members.

The job-creation activities reflect attempts to counteract the effects of macroeconomic policies demanded by the U.S. government and by U.S.-dominated international financial institutions like the International Monetary Fund. Such policies include privatization of government enterprises, cutbacks in government services, reduced or eliminated subsidies on basic goods, and other measures with negative consequences for workers. Governments around the world are being required to implement policies like these in order to become eligible for financial assistance and loans. The AALC has clearly affirmed its intention to provide a counterweight to these requirements:

> The IMF has prescribed certain draconian measures to be taken by African governments as a precondition for continued assistance and debt relief. These measures have resulted in even more unemployment as state-run industries undergo privatization and as government bureaucracies either lay off employees or stop hiring altogether...Trade union movements in many African countries have taken the lead in countering the effects of these measures, either through job creation projects, the development of cooperatives and credit unions or the direct assumption of responsibility for certain enterprises.[26]

Despite its criticisms of such "draconian" economic policies, the labor institute has helped to stabilize the macroeconomic structure by pacifying those most ill-treated by it. As part of its income-generation schemes the AALC has funded a vegetable gardening project in Botswana; labor-run banks, mines, and import-export companies in Zaire; cooperatives and credit unions in Zambia; and a women's vocational education project to train secretaries in Guinea.[27]

In Niger, the African institute supports a farm for former civil servants who lost their jobs due to cutbacks. The farm produces adobe bricks for housing, as well as rice, millet, sorghum, and vegetables. The project was described by the AALC as a "prototype which can serve as an example in Niger and elsewhere in West Africa, where workers are losing their jobs because of reductions in the numbers of civil servants and the increasing privatization of state enterprises."[28]

The institute's contention that the project of transplanting bureaucrats to farms should act as a "model" for counteracting the harsh effects of freewheeling capitalism ill serves the world's workers. On the contrary, it exemplifies the AFL-CIO's willingness to back U.S. foreign policy and the wishes of big business and financial institutions even when they conflict with workers' interests. What is worse, both U.S. labor and its overseas allies are diverting precious resources of time, material, and energy into schemes like these, rather than mounting principled and organized opposition to the austerity measures and restructuring formulas themselves.

Winning Minds Through Visitor Exchanges and Publications

Through publications and international visitor exchanges, the AFL-CIO participates in the global war of ideas. There is no question that these two activities also provide a useful service for overseas unionists. Union publications funded by the institutes, for instance, may report on issues such as minimum wage battles, organizing efforts, and strike activities. International exchanges help to transmit new ideas and forge alliances useful for expanding and strengthening global solidarity. But these institute activities also spread a doctrine of unionism compatible with the expansion of the U.S. economic and political sphere of influence.

International visitor exchanges, for instance, serve many purposes for the AFL-CIO and its government allies. They help to promote a worldview and develop skills compatible with the U.S. economic and political system. Meetings with media and government representatives, as well as with unionists and members of other private organizations lay the groundwork for alliances between foreign labor and important political actors in the United States. Such alliances can facilitate U.S. government and corporate expansion overseas by providing contact points with pro-U.S. unionists for U.S. government and business leaders.

A propaganda function is also served. Visits to the United States by U.S.-backed foreign unionists have helped to shape public opinion in this country about the political character of foreign governments and the "proper" role for the United States to play in international affairs. Other international visits—say to countries or conferences in Europe or Latin America—help frame the terms of debate in those regions as well. In the process, U.S. foreign policy is implicitly justified and promoted.

During the 1980s, for example, a central focus of AIFLD's NED-funded exchange program was "to bring to the attention of the international free trade union movement the issues at stake in the struggle for peace, democracy and economic progress in Central America."[29] Both top and midlevel labor delegations from the United States made repeated trips to Central America, especially to El Salvador and Nicaragua, to meet with AIFLD-backed unions and discuss political events there. Similarly, representatives from those countries came to the United States to present their cases to U.S. unions, the media, and Congress. There was an international dimension to the exchanges as well. For instance, three women from the Confederation of Trade Union Unity, an anti-Sandinista Nicaraguan confederation supported by AIFLD, were sent to the United Nations' "Decade on Women" conference in Kenya to "counter the presence of the official Sandinista delegation."[30]

Backing up propaganda-linked visitor exchanges are publications put out by the institutes. A 1983 report prepared by AIFLD's William Doherty entitled *Nicaragua, A Revolution Betrayed: Free*

Labor Persecuted was especially influential.[31] The 12-page report contained 29 allegations of Sandinista repression of "free" Nicaraguan unions and was used by the Reagan administration to win congressional approval of funds for the contras.

In response, the National Lawyers Guild in New York conducted its own fact-finding mission and produced a 62-page reply. "Virtually every claim of trade union repression made in the AIFLD report is disputed by representatives of the [AIFLD-backed Nicaraguan unions], by respected human rights groups, or by credible evidence provided by the Nicaraguan government," the lawyers reported.[32]

AIFLD publications critical of the Sandinistas continued throughout the 1980s and into the 1990s, each demonstrating the same haphazard relationship with the truth. Even Omar Baca Castillo, a member of the Confederation of Trade Union Unity, confessed to a progressive U.S. labor delegation that "Our international friends [at AIFLD] sometimes exaggerate the situation here." Observing that the institute was kicked out of the country in 1983, Baca explained, "AIFLD was creating many problems for us. Their last director in Nicaragua was making statements on his own for the CUS. He almost provoked a split. It didn't matter to us that they kicked AIFLD out."[33]

Besides promoting international visits and producing their own publications, the labor institutes have helped purchase office and press equipment, paid for the production and distribution of foreign union publications, and trained union journalists. Unions in South Africa, Indonesia, Nicaragua, Portugal, and Hungary have been among those who have received grants for such programs. During the years leading up to the collapse of the Soviet Union, the labor institute was actively boosting the anti-government media activities of nationalist unions in the Soviet republics and the Baltic states. With the demise of the Soviet bloc, such projects are continuing in an attempt to completely eradicate class-based analyses and substitute procapitalist ideas.

The media supported by the AFL-CIO's regional institutes disseminate an anticommunist perspective that bolsters Washington's foreign policy interests. The French publication *Social and Labor Studies* is subsidized by the Free Trade Union Institute with grants from the National Endowment for Democracy. The journal focuses on the activities of "communist-dominated trade unions" and international worker rights. In the Philippines, the Trade Union Congress of the Philippines receives NED grants through AAFLI to purchase office and press equipment and train union journalists. The objective, according to the endowment, is to "counteract left-wing propaganda." In 1984, AIFLD used NED funding to produce a series of manuals for regional labor education programs. They focused on political action and the debt crisis, as well as topics such as the "democratic process, totalitarianism, and the less absolute forms of dictatorship found throughout the region." Likewise, in Poland, the Free Trade Union Institute is using AID grant money—funneled through NED—to support the Foundation for Education for Democracy's efforts to introduce "democratic concepts and institutional reforms" in the schools.

Mobilizing the Masses Through Political Action

Because of the strategic importance of labor in political and economic arenas, grants funneled through the AFL-CIO's international institutes are used to support political action overseas. The institutes' allied unions abroad have been mobilized in attempts to stabilize and legitimize governments backed by Washington. Alternatively, they have hit the streets and the polls to oust governments opposed by the U.S. government. According to the Free Trade Union Institute's former executive director, Eugenia Kemble, "The basic point [of FTUI's support for foreign unions] is to build interest groups capable of shaping public policy in other countries."[34]

Using NED grants, the labor institutes finance various types of electoral activities around the world. These include civic education courses, technical assistance for setting up and administering political wings of the unions, voter registration drives, get-out-the-vote campaigns, media efforts, and related activities. "Political education committees" have been set up with institute funding in unions in Guatemala, Honduras, Panama, and the Dominican Republic. Unions in Chile, El Salvador, Haiti, Guatemala, Nicaragua, Botswana, the Philippines, and Eastern Europe have been among those to participate in institute programs with a specifically electoral focus.

In Nicaragua, the Confederation of Trade Union Unity and its allies in the Permanent Workers Congress (CPT) received NED support through AIFLD for their anti-Sandinista activities prior to the February 1990 elections. As part of these efforts, a "special cadre training program" was conducted for "selected" CPT leaders. They attended classes in political action and voter participation at the George Meany Center in Maryland and the Labor University of the Venezuelan Workers Confederation in Caracas.

"Cadre development programs" inside Nicaragua supplemented the foreign training and reached other workers throughout the country. The unionists were mobilized for demonstrations, voter registration efforts, get-out-the-vote drives, and other actions that implicitly promoted the candidacy of Violeta Chamorro and the National Opposition Union (UNO). Following the elections—in which Chamorro was victorious—the U.S.-backed labor sectors were targeted for further aid from the United States in order to contest the progressive leadership of the Nicaraguan labor movement.

A 1990 internal NED document discussing the post-election funding of the Nicaraguan trade unions described the priority placed on union efforts:

> There is a danger that the democratic process will be undermined by post-election events. After having suppressed strikes for years, some Sandinista trade unionists now threaten mass political strikes to 'protect the gains of the revolution.' A successful organizing drive by independent trade unionists aimed at creating a viable democratic presence in communities and industries throughout Nicaragua is crucial to maintaining a stable transition period.[35]

As in Nicaragua, directly partisan activities have been assisted by grants from the labor institutes in a number of countries. Revelations that the Panamanian Confederation of Workers used FTUI funds to campaign for the military-backed candidate in 1984 stimulated a flurry of criticism.[36] In response, Eugenia Kemble, then head of FTUI, said, "We did not think it was fair, or in the interest of democracy, to tell the union that as a condition of getting assistance from us to teach their members about political activity and to develop training programs and canvassing and so on, that the union not endorse a candidate."[37] Even after the fiasco in Panama—which stimulated the outrage of the U.S. ambassador—FTUI continued to award grants to unions which endorsed candidates. As Kemble described it, "The kind of training and voter activism that we started there [in Panama] is the kind of thing we still do. We did it in the Philippines. In Peru the union did take a position, and we had a training program there."[38]

During the recent upheavals in Eastern Europe, the Free Trade Union Institute fed financial resources and technical assistance to its labor allies. This support allowed Eastern European union federations such as Bulgaria's Podkrepa and Poland's Solidarity to mount their historic campaigns against the communist governments and to prepare for subsequent elections. In Bulgaria, Podkrepa and the NED-backed Union of Democratic Forces led mass demonstrations that helped topple the government of the Bulgarian Socialist Party (the reformed communist party), a government that had been legitimately elected in a multiparty contest in June 1990. The leaders of Podkrepa revealed to the *Los Angeles Times* that "the determination" of the anticommunist coalition was "bolstered by American solidarity and implied promises of better times to come."[39] Oleg Tchulev, Podkrepa's vice president, said that U.S. advisers and diplomats had provided the union with funding "sent through private channels, such as the AFL-CIO, which has sent computers, fax machines and advisers to help the trade union get organized and gain strength."[40]

In Bulgaria as in the rest of Eastern Europe, material assistance from the U.S. labor federation accelerated following the downfall of the old regimes. Now, however, the focus is on erecting western economic and political structures, revamping the educational system, and eroding the institutional remains of the previous regimes. The construction of pro-U.S. trade unions which will back planned radical economic restructuring in the region is a fundamental part of this process.

Such politicized activities have historical precedents. In the 1960s and 1970s, for instance, AIFLD-backed unions in the Dominican Republic, Guyana, and Chile were instrumental in efforts first to destabilize progressive governments and later to stabilize the reactionary regimes which took their place. This scenario was replayed in Grenada in 1984, when AIFLD provided NED grants to the Organization of Citizen Awareness for civic-education activities following the U.S. invasion the year before. The organization is a labor-initiated coalition of groups from different political and economic sectors. It used the grant money to conduct leadership trainings and target sectors such as young people in order to mobilize voters for participation in the elections.

There are many other examples of labor institute funding designed to stabilize pro-U.S. regimes. The Trade Union Congress of the Philippines has received U.S. funding through NED and AAFLI to shore up the government of Corazón Aquino. Likewise, U.S.-funded unions in South Korea, Zaire, and Indonesia—all notorious for repressive labor policies—have been maintained as relatively passive institutions whose activities are almost strictly apolitical and shop-floor oriented. Whether by intent, oversight, or hapless planning, the result is a de facto endorsement of the anti-union stances of those governments.

Building Buddy Unions Overseas

The union-building programs sponsored by the AFL-CIO's institutes bolster labor organizations that shun radical political and economic change and tend to focus on shop-floor issues like wages and fringe benefits. Assistance is provided for just about everything needed by a union, including office equipment, technical training, and salaries. But the AFL-CIO has created and strengthened these conservative unions at the expense of more broad-based and progressive labor groups. It has attempted to undercut and discredit militant unions in an effort to subject foreign labor to the control and influence of the United States.

A few examples illustrate the range of institution-building programs backed by the labor institutes. In Liberia, the African institute provided fuel, transportation, lodging, materials, and press coverage to support the Liberia Federation of Labour Unions in its efforts to organize workers in outlying areas. The Bangladesh Free Trade Union Congress used AAFLI grants to rent its office space and purchase office equipment. Similar programs paid for developing organizing, youth, and community service components for the Chilean Democratic Central of Workers and a technical assistance center for a Uruguayan union federation. In Nicaragua, following the election victory of the U.S.-backed UNO coalition, NED made a grant of $107,833 to FTUI for an organizing drive of pro-UNO unions to strengthen them during the three-month transition period before UNO officially took office. Infrastructure support was also provided to unions in Bulgaria, Czechoslovakia, Romania, and the Soviet Union during 1990.

In the Fiji islands, AAFLI supported the Fiji Trades Union Congress (FTUC) in an effort to undermine antinuclear initiatives opposed by Washington. Over the years, AAFLI has provided the FTUC with various types of aid, including travel grants, infrastructure support, and training. Its major efforts occurred in 1984, however, when the U.S. institute opened an office in Fiji as part of a campaign to defeat the nuclear-free Pacific resolution advanced by the Pacific Trade Union Forum. Documents released under the Freedom of Information Act revealed that AAFLI spent $1 million on the effort and claimed credit for defeat of the resolution.[41]

In a funding request to NED in 1986, the Asian institute's paternalistic commentary exposed the anticommunist lens through which it viewed South Pacific realities. It also highlighted the strategic significance of AAFLI's support for South Pacific labor organizations:

> The trade unions of the island nations of the South Pacific are fragile institutions...their ability to see distinctions between the Soviet bloc and the democratic nations of the world is sometimes clouded, especially when emotional issues such as colonialism, nuclear testing, and economic protection zones are introduced into the discussion...With the exceptions of political parties, these trade union organizations are the largest mass organs in their countries.[42]

Fiji is not the only Pacific island nation that has experienced AAFLI's meddling in its political affairs. The Asian institute also attempted to influence voting in the Philippine Senate to decide the fate of U.S. military bases in the country. In September 1991, mainstream Philippine newspapers, including the *Philippine Daily Globe*, the *Philippine Daily Inquirer*, and the *Manila Times*, disclosed that the U.S. institute had plans to funnel cash to sway key labor leaders. Ernesto Herrera, a senator as well as the TUCP's general secretary, had said in July 1991 that it would "be extremely difficult" to vote in favor of extending the treaty allowing the U.S. military to be based on the islands. Herrera, whose labor congress represents many of the 70,000 workers at the Clark and Subic Bay bases, said the treaty showed "almost a contemptuous disregard of Filipino workers' interest."[43] But Herrera later switched his vote, admitting that in exchange the TUCP had received a pledge of $3.7 million from AAFLI and a promise of another $10 million from Richard Armitage, the chief U.S. negotiator of the bases agreement. The money was described as "bases compensation." When the offers were publicized by Philippine newspapers on the eve of the vote, the pledges were revoked.[44] At least one other labor official, Paterno Menzon of the Independent Labor Alliance of Workers, was also offered money if he switched from an anti-bases position and took a stand in favor of the agreement. Menzon said that outgoing U.S. labor attaché James Murphy and AAFLI official Tom Riley offered him 30,000 pesos per month (more than $1100 in U.S. terms) if he would switch his position on the bases and affiliate his labor alliance with the TUCP.[45]

Accusations that the AFL-CIO has sabotaged labor unity and promoted reformist, manipulated unions at the expense of larger and more militant labor organizations have been repeated so often they are basic truisms. As far back as the 1960s, Victor Reuther, then director of international affairs for the United Auto Workers, blasted the AFL-CIO for supporting "small and unrepresentative" groups of unions, while ignoring larger and more democratic ones.[46] In 1977, the Nigerian government found that the African institute had pumped so much money into the United Labor Congress of Nigeria to prop it up vis-à-vis the leftwing Nigerian Trades Union Congress that foreigners had effective control of the organization.[47]

In El Salvador, perhaps the most notorious recent case, the decade of the 1980s witnessed a string of AIFLD attempts to split militant labor organizations, peel away more cooperative members, create U.S.-controlled alternatives, and then promote their creations as the true spokespersons for Salvadoran labor.[48] The results—assassination, torture, arbitrary arrest, and other official harassment of non-AIFLD unionists—provide a tragic example of the effects of the AFL-CIO's strategy of promoting "moderate" unionists in hopes of undercutting those the U.S. federation feels are vulnerable to communist influence. It is also a country in which the AFL-CIO's approach stands naked in its hypocrisy. Lane Kirkland, writing in 1983, explained an essential component of the federation's philosophy that supposedly guided its activities overseas:

> Experience teaches us...that free and strong trade unions are the most effective instrument for improving wages and working conditions. Experience has also taught us that such unions cannot flourish except in a climate of respect for human rights...
>
> Of all the commonly enumerated human rights, we believe the most important is freedom of association...Freedom of association means, simply, the right of ordinary people who share common interests to form their own institutions in order to advance those interests and to shelter them against the arbitrary power of the state, the employer, or other strongholds of self-interest. Absent such sheltering institutions, not only are the people powerless to defend such other rights as they may have against state encroachment, but those rights are inevitably attenuated. Freedom of speech is reduced to the right to cry alone in the wilderness; freedom of worship is restricted to solitary meditation; and freedom of assembly is, literally, pointless. Effective political opposition—and therefore democracy itself—is impossible.[49]

But in El Salvador, despite Kirkland's inspiring rhetoric, the U.S. institute has relentlessly undermined militant labor organizations that oppose the U.S.-backed government. Classified documents from the U.S. embassy in San Salvador confirmed both AIFLD's role in splitting the Salvadoran union movement and official U.S. backing for such efforts. As reported in the *Nation* in 1987, the documents showed that some of AIFLD's $3.5 million 1986 budget for operations in El Salvador was used to lure the Popular Democratic Unity (UPD) away from participation in the National Unity of Salvadoran Workers (UNTS), a broad-based coalition sympathetic to radical reform.

The UPD was an umbrella organization of rural and urban groups linked to the U.S. labor institute, which was instrumental in organizing the UPD back in 1980. In 1984, the UPD helped promote the candidacy of Christian Democrat José Napoleón Duarte, the presidential candidate favored by Washington and the leadership of the AFL-CIO. When Duarte did not come through on essential campaign pledges, however, the UPD helped form the UNTS.

But AIFLD, with embassy support, moved to tear the new coalition apart. One document revealed that UPD head Ramon Mendoza received a payment of $3000 as "initial assistance" for pulling his organization out of the UNTS. Another memorandum urged AIFLD to "direct its policy at holding our side together, while continuing to pick off U.N.T.S. member unions one-by-one."[50]

Salvadoran workers have felt the heat generated by such policies. Adrian Esquino, an Indian campesino leader in El Salvador, denounced the labor institute after his union lost its AIFLD funding, radio, and jeep because it refused to affiliate with a new AIFLD-backed confederation. "AIFLD is a disaster for workers," Esquino charged. "AIFLD says if you do what we want, we'll give you money. The institute buys union leaders."[51]

CHAPTER FIVE
Prospects for Real Solidarity:
Contradictions and Cross-Pressures

With its global network, its multiple ties to the U.S. government, and the continued dominance of its conservative hierarchy, the AFL-CIO seems well-positioned to continue business as usual in its international operations. Yet the future of the AFL-CIO's foreign policy and its status as the vanguard democracy-intervention organization are uncertain. Contradictory influences are at work which could either shift the federation in more progressive directions or reinforce the status quo.

Both at home and abroad, the federation is operating in a more complex political environment. The internationalization of the economy is laying waste to the notion that U.S. workers necessarily profit from the overseas adventures of U.S. corporations. Likewise, the contradictions of the AFL-CIO's alliance with government and business are chickens which are coming home to roost in the form of assaults on the material status of workers both in the United States and overseas. A rank-and-file attack on some aspects of the AFL-CIO's foreign policy, increasingly independent stances taken by some of its overseas affiliates, and the breakup of the Soviet bloc have all undermined the traditional foundations of the AFL-CIO's policies overseas.

In addition to these influences, labor no longer stands alone as the sole vanguard of the "democracy-building" strategy. It now shares the field with a multitude of other players, ranging from business associations to women's organizations. Moreover, fiscal pressures on Washington have clamped off budgetary increases for the labor institutes. Overall AID funding to labor has decreased over the last few years. The National Endowment for Democracy has made up the shortfall, but the institutes are not finding their budgets swollen with massive funding increases, at least for regional core programs. Even so, some of their commitments are expanding—to Eastern Europe and the states of the former Soviet Union, for example—and many of these initiatives are specifically requested by Washington and come with earmarked funding.

Meanwhile, the U.S. government is committing itself ever more completely to the use of private organizations to intervene "overtly" overseas, and labor still has the most far-flung network and time-tested expertise of all the groups now performing government-funded activities abroad. Moreover, its links to the U.S. government and to the increasingly important intervention network are firm. Labor is still a strategic sector for economic and political reasons, if not for Cold War purposes.

All these factors produce cross-pressures on the AFL-CIO whose outcomes are unpredictable. There is, however, a "window of opportunity" through which progressive labor might launch a new foreign policy, working both within and outside of the labor federation. Rising from the grassroots, such a foreign policy would seek international labor unity and social justice—not the expansion of a U.S. sphere of influence which is proving less and less hospitable to workers both in the United States and overseas.

Diminished Returns from U.S. Imperialism

The decline of the United States as an economic power, coupled with the internationalization of capital and the growing power of transnational corporations (TNCs) have eroded U.S. labor's position in the global economy.[1] TNCs take advantage of and try to perpetuate low wage levels and labor repression in the third world in order to increase their profits and reduce their social responsibilities to labor. The resulting phenomenon of runaway shops has fueled job loss, declining wage levels, employment insecurity, and threats to trade union rights in the developed world. "American workers," according to one analyst, "have been plunged into a cold bath of global competition."[2]

The hemorrhage of well-paid U.S. manufacturing jobs to assembly shops overseas has stripped traditional AFL-CIO foreign policy of two of its major underpinnings. New resources secured by U.S. imperial advances such as the war in the Persian Gulf do not necessarily translate into enhanced productivity, an expanding job market, or job security in the United States. Instead, U.S.-based transnational corporations may utilize such resources to fuel production in their plants overseas. The TNCs reap profits from these resources and productive facilities that do not return to the U.S. worker in the form of increased wages and benefits, but in the form of consumer imports for which they must pay increasingly large portions of their shrinking paychecks. In addition, the continued repression of third world workers, often at starvation wages under intolerable working conditions, impedes the development of markets overseas for goods produced by U.S. labor.

Aside from these problems inherent in the traditional support of the AFL-CIO for U.S. expansionism and global capitalism, there are deep-seated contradictions manifested by labor's support of Washington-backed union programs while other government funding explicitly promotes social sectors and macroeconomic policies that hurt workers. Through the Center for International Private Enterprise, the National Republican Institute for International Affairs, and an assortment of other government and nongovernmental agencies, the National Endowment for Democracy and entities like AID are promoting economic and political forces that favor business interests over those of workers.

In El Salvador, for example, a Salvadoran business group funded by AID ran an advertisement in *Bobbin,* a clothing industry trade magazine, that showed an attractive young woman working quietly at a sewing machine. The advertisement pulled back the covers on the strange bedfellows of the AFL-CIO in its government-funded overseas activities:

> Rosa Martinez produces apparel for U.S. markets on her sewing machine in El Salvador. You can hire her for 57-cents an hour.
>
> Rosa is more than just colorful. She and her co-workers are known for their industriousness, reliability and quick learning. They make El Salvador one of the best buys in the [Caribbean Basin Initiative].[3]

Most of the organizations funded by agencies like NED and AID advocate free-market, neoliberal economic strategies. Frequently such strategies directly harm workers, especially those in the third world. For instance, privatization of publicly owned enterprises and cutbacks in government-sponsored social services lead to a loss of jobs, declining wages, and reduced or eliminated subsidies on basics like food, medical care, utilities, heating fuel, and transportation.

Similarly, when import duties are lowered, domestic economies become vulnerable to increased foreign economic penetration and competition. These influences often lead to weakening or closure of domestic enterprises, with a subsequent reduction in wage levels and benefits, tightened labor restrictions, and even job loss. In like manner, deregulation negatively affects workers in both the developed countries and the third world. It weakens important safeguards such as occupational health and safety provisions and can lead to the reduction or elimination of various social welfare benefits provided by employers.

Such policies are being pressed by Washington and its business allies across the world, and the labor institutes of the AFL-CIO are providing implicit backing to them. In Africa and Eastern Europe, for instance, both of which have been especially hard hit by such policies, the AFL-CIO is promoting job-creation schemes and volunteer efforts to soften the blow. A more effective strategy for labor would require the federation to mount a full-scale analysis and rejection of such policies. Although the AFL-CIO has made some attempts in this direction, particularly in its analysis of the international debt, its efforts have been primarily rhetorical. Most significantly, the federation and its institutes have adopted band-aid solutions such as job-creation schemes but have avoided mobilizing workers for political actions against neoliberal policies and the national and international forces which advance them.

Ironically, this is the case even though the federation recognizes the problems for workers of an increasingly integrated global economy. As observed by AFL-CIO President Kirkland in 1983,

> American workers have a vested self-interest in the improvement of wages and working conditions in other countries. They cannot compete with workers earning 50 or 75 cents an hour; nor can such wages generate the purchasing power to sustain markets for American exports. And with the proliferation of multinational corporations, organized workers in the United States need counterpart workers' organizations abroad with which they can develop common strategies in response to common problems.[4]

Even with this recognition, however, the AFL-CIO hierarchy has had difficulty jettisoning old ideas about the world in order to keep pace with rapid global economic and political transformations. "The top leadership of the federation is full of bureaucrats," observed one activist on Central America labor issues. "They kill activism even if they're not ideologically committed to killing it." Another activist questioned whether the federation's staff in the international affairs department would be capable of escaping from the Cold War straitjacket that has shaped postwar labor programs. "These guys have become appendages of the U.S. defense system," the unionist declared. "We [in the rank and file] don't like what they're doing in foreign policy."

Rebellion in the Ranks

Sentiments like these have stimulated increasing opposition to the AFL-CIO hierarchy and its foreign policy both within the federation and among its associates overseas. During the 1980s—spurred by crises in Central America and South Africa—the U.S. rank and file's willingness to accept foreign policy stands enunciated by the AFL-CIO eroded significantly. In a historic shift, conflicts over the AFL-CIO's foreign policy positions in Central America were pushed to the floor of the 1985 convention in Anaheim, California. For the first time ever, disagreements which were normally hashed out behind the scenes exploded in floor debates which directly challenged the AFL-CIO's executive officers over the conduct of the federation and its institutes abroad.[5]

Over the past few years, this increasingly savvy opposition from rank-and-file and midlevel labor officials in the United States has set some limits—moderate and irregular, to be sure, but hard-won and extremely important, nonetheless—on the freedom of movement of the AFL-CIO in some countries overseas.[6] For instance, in convention fights after 1985, labor activists obtained compromise resolutions that distanced the AFL-CIO from support for contra aid. As a result, the progressive labor movement was able to throw its official weight behind calls to Congress for a cutoff of aid and to join mobilizations with other movements in opposition to U.S. policy in Central America. Such efforts were significant in the 1988 congressional defeat of contra aid legislation.

Based on the success of opposition such as this, the AFL-CIO's hierarchy's usually complete hegemony over the federation's foreign policy is no longer secure and may be at its most vulnerable of any time during the postwar period. If internal union opposition to the hierarchy's decision-making remains steadfast, these progressive unionists might force some major changes in overall policy in the long run. As it is, their dedicated efforts pushed the hierarchy to seek El Salvador's inclusion on the U.S. government's list of countries to be excluded from special trade privileges on the basis of its labor rights violations. In addition, local labor committees during the 1980s organized campaigns in solidarity with foreign unionists over official AFL-CIO objection, established "sister-union" relationships with shunned Salvadoran and Nicaraguan unions, collected material aid, and organized conferences attacking official AFL-CIO policies abroad.[7]

These pressures plus the changing international realities have led to some important changes in the official policies of the federation. "There's a change in the AFL-CIO stance, at least in Mexico," says one labor analyst. "Before [the decline of U.S. economic power], the AFL would support policies good for U.S. corporations on the assumption that that strategy would benefit U.S. workers. Now there is a move to support workers in the third world because of the need to shore up labor's position in the United States."

The renegade activities of some AFL-CIO allies overseas also alters the playing field for the federation's foreign policy. As neatly stated by one observer, "'[T]rade union imperialism' must be seen in context and with a view to its effectiveness rather than simply its intentions."[8] With this as the criterion, the record of the AFL-CIO's international institutes is clearly mixed. The labor federation certainly attempts to influence and manipulate its affiliates overseas. It has created or supported domesticated, probusiness union movements around the world. But its capacity to influence actual labor trends in any given country over the long term is subject to local factors, such as class relationships, historical antagonisms in the society, the extent of government repression, and the intensity of worker exploitation. The federation has also had little long-range effectiveness in large countries with already developed and independent labor movements, such as the Southern Cone nations of South America.

In response to these purely indigenous factors, workers across the world who find their material interests not well-served by U.S.-backed unions have radicalized their unions or mobilized new labor organizations which aggressively pursue both political and shop-floor agendas.[9] As the case of the TUCP in the Philippines attests, buying off foreign unionists with U.S. trainings, attractive social services, and low-interest loans certainly lures new members to pro-U.S. unions backed by the AFL-CIO's institutes. In the long run, however, those unions may lose their appeal, particularly if they are too docile in the face of exploitation and repression.

El Salvador offers an excellent example of this phenomenon. There, despite the dependence of the country on the United States and the fragility of the labor movement, AIFLD had to create three and abandon two confederations between 1980 and 1986. In each case the institute's offspring grew increasingly obstreperous as important leaders and members of the rank and file realized their interests were being undermined by their alliance with AIFLD and the U.S.-backed government.[10] At the beginning of the 1990s, there are rumblings of a similar break between AIFLD and its latest creation in El Salvador, the National Union of Workers and Campesinos.

In South Africa, the largest and most powerful union confederation, the Congress of South African Trade Unions (COSATU), has grown steadily in power and stature throughout the 1980s. Its tactical sophistication and clarity of purpose has allowed it to remain independent from the AFL-CIO despite repeated overtures from the U.S. federation. After the ban on the African National Congress (ANC) was lifted, the AFL-CIO stepped up its advances to the ANC-linked federation. Moving into 1991, analysts believe that there will almost certainly be some type of relationship hammered out between the U.S. federation and COSATU. But the African union organization is operating from a position of strength vis-à-vis the AFL-CIO and its African institute. Although it needs the resources offered by the U.S. federation, COSATU is unlikely to be bought off or tamed by the United States, according to these analysts.[11] The National Security Archive's Kenneth Mokoena predicted that the U.S. labor federation will "not have a rousing success in South Africa" because "COSATU is strong and sophisticated; it will have its own agenda to lay on the AALC."

Building the Future

With the breakup of the Soviet bloc and the consequent unraveling of its international labor arm—the World Federation of Trade Unions—the U.S. labor institutes are facing an evaporating enemy. The concept of promoting "free," (i.e. anticommunist and pro-U.S.) unions is rapidly becoming outdated and irrelevant. As one top union staffer described it, "With the collapse of communism, the AFL's fig leaf is gone. The rationale which they used to justify their activities has been removed." The challenge at this point is to develop worldwide linkages among workers to combat an exploitative international division of labor which keeps workers competing with each other rather than confronting the economic and political structures that produce exploitation. "We all have the same hard life," a foreign unionist explained. "We are bound together by one string."[12]

Unless there is a major shift at the leadership levels of the AFL-CIO, however, the labor institutes are unlikely to rise to this important task. As it is, they continue to promote U.S. national interests over those of their natural constituencies, while declining to ally themselves with the most progressive and militant sectors of labor. In these ways they perpetuate the expansion of U.S. power and, in the process, debilitate workers around the world.

What is needed therefore is the further development of the rank-and-file foreign policy and accompanying strategies whose broad outlines have been drawn over the last decade. An increasing sense of internationalism has characterized this emerging foreign policy. A 1990 conference of unionists referred to it as a "one-world strategy" which mimics the global corporate strategies of the TNCs.[13] Held in Miami under the auspices of the International Federation of Chemical, Energy and General Workers' Unions—an influential ITS—the meeting involved unionists from chemical, energy, and rubber unions in 30 countries. The "one-world strategy" elaborated at the meeting treats the world as an interconnected and interdependent whole, emphasizing the common needs and shared fates of workers around the world.

Cross-national linkages in pursuit of sharply elevated conditions for workers everywhere, as well as an analysis of the diminished importance for labor of nationalism in an age of TNC dominance are components of this new foreign policy.[14]

Ron Blackwell, an economist with the Amalgamated Clothing and Textile Workers Union, has participated in the development of this new vision. "We recognize that international economic integration will continue, and that wages and working conditions will equalize," Blackwell explains. "The task is to build international worker solidarity to assure that wages and working conditions tend to equalize at a higher rather than a lower level."[15]

This objective requires workers to join hands in efforts to shape the emerging international economy, not just react to it. Joint international actions to promote adoption and enforcement of a single international code of conduct for transnational corporations is one element of this strategy. Such a code, according to the unionists involved in formulating it, would outline corporate responsibilities not only to labor, but also regarding environmental issues and similar concerns for society at large. Joe Uhlein, a representative of the AFL-CIO's Industrial Union Department, described fundamental components of such a code:

> The code would be enforceable whenever a corporation, its agents, or its property entered, operated in, or left a country. The code might require corporations to report investment intentions upon entering a country and disclose any hazardous materials imported. It might forbid employment of children or environmental discharge of pollutants. It might require companies closing an operation to provide advance notification and severance pay. The code would include a 'neutrality clause' under which a company would agree as a matter of corporate policy not to oppose union organizing in its plants, branches, or subsidiaries in any country.[16]

Even more important, however, is the long-range objective of such actions: to create a global environment supportive of the individuals whose labor keeps the world's economic wheels in motion and whose lives must be lived out in the surroundings ground down by those wheels. To create such an environment, it is necessary to end the false competition between "privileged" workers in developed countries and impoverished workers in the third world, or between "communist" and "anticommunist" unionists. The current competition—fueled by underdevelopment and labor repression in the third world and a misguided call for labor-business "harmony" in the developed capitalist countries—drags wages down and undermines worker rights everywhere. The new labor foreign policy aims to link workers around the world in a common front to press for their demands against government and business.

These international bonds are made possible in part by the communications revolution.[17] From fax machines to electronic mail and even satellite links, new communications technology has the potential to join otherwise isolated unionists in a web of information and coordinated solidarity actions. It has already facilitated coordinated action for a variety of U.S. unions confronting foreign companies and their anti-union efforts in this country.[18] Because such networks are relatively inexpensive, these communications hook-ups also have the potential to democratize labor's foreign policy by breaking the hold of the AFL-CIO hierarchy on information about foreign affairs.

In addition to a renewed emphasis on internationalism, the foreign policy being constructed by progressive labor over the past decade has attempted to break down divisions among groups within national boundaries. It has been marked by the cooperation of exploited and oppressed groups and their supporters throughout multiple sectors of society. From churches to trade unions, from women's groups to ethnically-based organizations, from homeless advocacy groups to associations promoting an end to the arms race, boundaries have been breaking down and linkages developing among diverse groups with a common desire to increase equity and social justice both nationally and internationally.[19] The 1990 labor strategizing meeting in Miami called for just such a strengthening of the ties between labor unions, the community, and environmental groups.

Utilizing international labor structures such as the ITS and ad hoc cross-union coalitions, unionists have mounted joint efforts to force companies to redress worker grievances in places as far distant as Central America, South Africa, South Korea, and the United States. They have also joined in activities which, on their face, are more explicitly political in objective. In response to the U.S. war in the Persian Gulf, for example, labor councils and unions around the country passed resolutions calling for negotiated solutions. Their participation amplified and refined the protests of other antiwar organizations by articulating the negative effects on labor of war in the Gulf. They also spotlighted the self-interest of U.S. transnational corporations as a factor in the country's war fever.[20]

Such international and intersectoral coalitions are antidotes to the divisive approach to labor pursued by the AFL-CIO since the end of World War II. With the demise of the Cold War, redbaiting progressive unionists will be less effective as a strategy to divide and conquer the world's labor movements in the interests of U.S. empire-building. As the "new world order" falls into place, there is an opportunity for progressive unionists to blow away the AFL-CIO's anticommunist smokescreen and point out the damage done to workers by a global capitalism more interested in the pursuit of profits than in the pursuit of equity. A shrinking world and an increasingly transnational economic system offer the best postwar opportunity ever to set aside the damaging assumptions of the AFL-CIO's foreign policy and get on with the business of building truly global solidarity among the world's workers.

Appendix A:
A Sampler of AFL-CIO Projects Worldwide

Country	Fiscal Year	Grant Award	U.S. Govt. Funding Agency	Description of Project
				Asian-American Free Labor Institute
Bangladesh	1989	$119,075	AID	union trainings, salary subsidies, family planning workshops, medical care, a rotating loan fund, and vocational training. According to AAFLI, in the tea plantations, "managers have begun to release workers as they modernize production methods on the estates. The result has been to reduce family incomes. This has made union-run schemes that generate income and/or make services available at a lower cost even more important."
Indonesia	1989	$43,000	AID	salary subsidies for three of six staff of the union newspaper *Media Pekerja,* as part of a "public opinion creation program"
Philippines	1990	$30,000	AID	to produce, direct, and air human rights radio dramas

Continued on following two pages

Country	Fiscal Year	Grant Award	U.S. Govt. Funding Agency	Description of Project
				African-American Labor Center
Sierra Leone	1989	Not given	AID	union institutional support, including vehicle maintenance and operation; preparation, duplication, distribution, and storage of educational materials; and administrative overhead
Zaire	1989	Not given	Not given	shipment of pharmaceuticals donated by Direct Relief Foundation
Zimbabwe	1989	Not given	AID	various projects, including an adult literacy program, institution of financial control system, seminars, and workshops
				American Institute for Free Labor Development
Chile	1977	$172,000	AID	to conduct local, national, and regional courses and seminars for urban and rural workers with an ultimate goal of creating a "generally apolitical, socially responsible [trade union movement] concerned with bread-and-butter interests of workers"
Nicaragua	1989	$65,430	NED	seed and fertilizer for campesino affiliates of CUS
Nicaragua	1990	$107,833	AID/NED	organizing drive for U.S.-backed unions "aimed at rapid expansion of their core of trained activists" during the strategic three months between the Feb. 1990 elections and the inauguration of Violeta Chamorro of the Washington-funded UNO coalition

Free Trade Union Institute

Country	Year		Source	Amount	Description
Bulgaria	1990		AID/NED	$276,190	to buy newsprint and communications and organizational equipment for the opposition trade union, Podkrepa
Czecho-slovakia	1990		NED	$10,000	to support "democratic strike committees"
Hungary	1990		Not given	$502,000	to assist the Democratic League of Independent Trade Unions in organizing pre-election voter education and participation activities
Portugal	1990		NED	$270,938	organizing and education activities of UGT in Portugal

Sources: AID, "FY 1990 Democratic Initiatives and Human Rights Program Summary," internal AID document, undated; AID, *Project Appraisal Report on AIFLD Project No. 598-0101 in Chile, April 1, 1976 - March 31, 1977*; AAFLI, *Asian-American Free Labor Institute Annual Report to AID, January 1, 1989 - December 3, 1989*, submitted June 30, 1990; AAFLI, *Program Submission to the Agency for International Development, Years 1989-90, 1990-91, 1991-92*, submitted January 18, 1989; AALC, *1989 Annual Report to AID for January 1 - December 31, 1989*, on Grant No. AFR-0441-A-00-5017-00, submitted March 1990; *AALC Reporter*, Vol. 24, No. 6, 1989; Minutes of the January 19, 1990 Meeting of the Board of Directors of the National Endowment for Democracy; Minutes of the March 29, 1990 Meeting of the Board of Directors of the National Endowment for Democracy; and *Free Trade Union Institute Quarterly Report to NED for July 1, 1989 - September 30, 1989*, submitted October 31, 1989.

Appendix B
Boards of Trustees and Executive Officers of the Institutes

Free Trade Union Institute

African-American Labor Center

Lane Kirkland, president
Thomas Donahue, secretary-treasurer
Patrick J. O'Farrell, executive director

Morton Bahr
Communications Workers of America

John J. Barry
International Brotherhood of Electrical Workers

William Bywater
International Union of Electrical Workers

Robert A. Georgine
Wood, Wire and Metal Lathers International Union

Wayne E. Glenn
United Paperworkers International Union

John T. Joyce
International Union of Bricklayers and Allied Craftsmen

Richard I. Kilroy
Brotherhood of Railway, Airlines and Steamship Clerks, Freight
Handlers, Express and Station Employees

Jay Mazur
International Ladies' Garment Workers Union

Lenore Miller
Retail, Wholesale and Department Store Union

Albert Shanker
American Federation of Teachers

John Sturdivant
American Federation of Government Employees

John J. Sweeney
Service Employees International Union

Lynn R. Williams
United Steelworkers of America

American Institute for Free Labor Development

Lane Kirkland, president
Albert Shanker, vice president
Thomas R. Donahue, secretary-treasurer
William Doherty, executive director

Morton Bahr
Communications Workers of America

Owen Bieber
United Auto Workers

William H. Bywater
International Union of Electrical Workers

Robert A. Georgine
Wood, Wire and Metal Lathers International Union

James E. Hatfield
Glass, Pottery, Plastics and Allied Workers International Union

John T. Joyce
International Union of Bricklayers and Allied Craftsmen

Richard I. Kilroy
Brotherhood of Railway, Airlines and Steamship Clerks, Freight Handlers, Express and Station Employees

Jay Mazur
International Ladies' Garment Workers Union

Joyce D. Miller
Amalgamated Clothing and Textiles Workers Union

John N. Sturdivant
American Federation of Government Employees

John J. Sweeney
Service Employees International Union

Lynn R. Williams
United Steelworkers of America

William H. Wynn
United Food and Commercial Workers International Union

Asian-American Free Labor Institute

Lane Kirkland, president
Thomas Donahue, secretary-treasurer
Charles D. Gray, executive director

Morton Bahr
Communications Workers of America

John J. Barry
International Brotherhood of Electrical Workers

John DeConcini
Bakery, Confectionary and Tobacco Workers International Union

Larry L. Dugan, Jr.
International Union of Operating Engineers

Angelo Fosco
Laborers' International Union of North America

John T. Joyce
International Union of Bricklayers and Allied Craftsmen

Richard I. Kilroy
Brotherhood of Railway, Airlines and Steamship Clerks, Freight Handlers, Express and Station Employees

Jay Mazur
International Ladies' Garment Workers Union

Gerald W. McEntee
American Federation of State, County and Municipal Employees

Joyce D. Miller
Amalgamated Clothing and Textile Workers Union

Lenore Miller
Retail, Wholesale and Department Store Union

Albert Shanker
American Federation of Teachers

John N. Sturdivant
American Federation of Government Employees

John J. Sweeney
Service Employees International Union

Lynn R. Williams
United Steelworkers of America

William H. Wynn
United Food and Commercial Workers International Union

List of Abbreviations

AAFLI	Asian-American Free Labor Institute
AALC	African-American Labor Center
AFL-CIO	American Federation of Labor-Congress of Industrial Organizations
AFRO	African Regional Organization
AFT	American Federation of Teachers
AID	Agency for International Development
AIFLD	American Institute for Free Labor Development
ANACH	National Association of Honduran Peasants
APRO	Asia-Pacific Regional Organization
AUDD	Agrarian Union Development Department
BATU	Brotherhood of Asian Trade Unions
CIA	Central Intelligence Agency
CLAT	Latin American Confederation of Workers
COSATU	Congress of South African Trade Unions
CPT	Permanent Workers Congress (Nicaragua)
CPUSTAL	Congress of Unified Trade Unions of Latin American Workers
CUS	Confederation of Trade Union Unity (Nicaragua)
CUSG	Confederation of Guatemalan Trade Union Unity
CVT	Vietnamese Confederation of Labor
CWA	Communications Workers of America
DIA	International Affairs Department
FKTU	Federation of Korean Trade Unions
FOS	Federation of Trade Union Workers (Haiti)
FTUC	Fiji Trades Union Congress
FTUI	Free Trade Union Institute
IAF	Inter-American Foundation
IESCA	Central American Institute for Labor Studies

ICFTU	International Confederation of Free Trade Unions
ILO	International Labor Organization
IRC	International Rescue Committee
ITS	International Trade Secretariat(s)
IUBAC	International Union of Bricklayers and Allied Craftsmen
IUF	International Union of Food and Allied Workers' Associations
IWW	Industrial Workers of the World
KMU	Kilusang Mayo Uno (May First Movement, Philippines)
KTUC	Korea Trade Union Congress
LAC/AID	Bureau for Latin America and the Caribbean
LID	League for Industrial Democracy
NED	National Endowment for Democracy
OATUU	Organization of African Trade Union Unity
OECD	Organization for Economic Cooperation and Development
ORIT	Interamerican Regional Organization of Workers
OSS	Office of Strategic Services
OTAC	Organization of Central African Workers
OTUWA	Organization of Trade Unions of West Africa
PAFL	Pan American Federation of Labor
PTTI	Postal, Telegraph and Telephone International
PRODEMCA	Friends of the Democratic Center in Central America
SATUCC	Southern Africa Trade Union Coordinating Council
SD/USA	Social Democrats, USA
SEIU	Service Employees International Union
SPSI	Indonesia Workers' Union
SWWU	Seamans' and Waterfront Workers' Union (Grenada)
TNC	Transnational Corporation
TUAC	Trade Union Advisory Committee
TUCP	Trade Union Congress of the Philippines
TUI	Trade Unions International
UNO	National Opposition Union (Nicaragua)
UNOC	National Union of Workers and Campesinos (El Salvador)
WCL	World Confederation of Labor
WFTU	World Federation of Trade Unions

Notes

Introduction

1. Jeremy Brecher and Tim Costello, "Labor Goes Global: Global Village vs. Global Pillage," *Z Magazine,* January 1991.

2. "Proposed Free Trade Agreement Will Harm U.S. Workers," *Texas AFL-CIO Labor News,* April 1991, p. 7.

3. The American Federation of Labor (AFL) and Congress of Industrial Organizations (CIO) merged in 1955 to become the preeminent labor confederation in the United States. Their merger culminated a process of bureaucratization and deradicalization of U.S. labor which achieved its greatest momentum following World War II. Over the years, radical and communist unions had been purged from the two confederations. At the same time, the U.S. government and corporations had become more accepting of the bread-and-butter unionism represented by the more conservative wings of the confederations. The CIO, which had been more independent of government and more militant than the AFL, capitulated to the combined pressures of the Cold War and the benefits of labor unity when it merged with its larger rival.

4. These include Gary K. Busch, *The Political Role of International Trades Unions* (London: MacMillan Press, 1983); Philip S. Foner, *U.S. Labor Movement and Latin America: A History of Workers' Response to Intervention Vol. 1, 1846-1919* (South Hadley, MA: Bergin & Garvey Publishers, Inc., 1988); Ronald Radosh, *American Labor and United States Foreign Policy* (New York: Random House, 1969); Hobart A. Spalding, Jr., "U.S. Labor Intervention in Latin America: The Case of the American Institute for Free Labor Development," in Roger Southall, ed., *Trade Unions and the New Industrialization of the Third World* (London: Zed Books, 1988); and Dave Spooner, *Partners or Predators: International Trade Unionism and Asia* (Hong Kong: Asia Monitor Resource Center, 1989). See also Tom Barry and Deb Preusch, *AIFLD in Central America: Agents as Organizers* (Albuquerque, NM: Inter-Hemispheric Education Resource Center, 1986).

5. Figures given in Tom Kahn, "Beyond Mythology: A Reply to Paul Garver," *Labor Research Review No. 13, Solidarity Across Borders: U.S.*

Labor in a Global Economy (Chicago: Midwest Center for Labor Research, Spring 1989).

6. "Unions Briefed on Red Goals," *Business Week,* May 15, 1966.

7. Like many of the other knowledgeable people with whom we spoke, this congressional staff person requested confidentiality. This individual acts as a top aide to a member of Congress deeply involved with issues affecting labor.

8. *The AFL-CIO's Foreign Policy,* AFL-CIO Publication No. 181 (Washington: AFL-CIO, 1987).

9. AFL-CIO, *Report to the 1989 Convention from the AFL-CIO Executive Council* (Washington: AFL-CIO, 1989), p. 250.

10. Dan La Botz, *The Crisis of Mexican Labor* (New York: Praeger, 1988), p. 1.

11. H.M. Gittelman defines business unionism as "that variety of trade unionism which limits its activities to servicing the *immediate* needs of its members through collective bargaining and political action, and without more than an indirect regard for the following: the structure of, or the distribution of power within, the society in which such unionism exists; the long range interests of union members, regardless of how those interests are defined; and the welfare of workers who do not belong to the organization, except for those who readily fall within the recognized jurisdiction of a union but have not yet been organized." H.M. Gittelman, "Adolf Strasser and the Origins of Pure and Simple Unionism," *Labor History,* No. 6, 1965, p. 72.

12. For a brief, readable, and informative look at this process in El Salvador, see Robert Armstrong, Hank Frundt, Hobart Spalding, and Sean Sweeney, *Working Against Us: The American Institute for Free Labor Development and the International Policy of the AFL-CIO* (New York: North American Congress on Latin America, undated).

13. National Labor Committee in Support of Democracy and Human Rights in El Salvador, *Worker Rights and the New World Order: El Salvador, Honduras, Guatemala* (New York, June 1991), p. 16.

14. See Daniel Cantor and Juliet Schor, *Tunnel Vision: Labor, The World Economy, and Central America* (Boston: South End Press, 1987) for a discussion of "Wall Street Internationalism" and the economic inducements which traditionally have undergirded much of the AFL-CIO's foreign policy.

15. Quoted in Lloyd C. Gardner, *Imperial America: American Foreign Policy Since 1898* (New York: Harcourt Brace Jovanovich, Inc., 1976), p. 17.

16. Quoted in Walter LaFeber, *The New Empire* (Ithaca, NY: Cornell University Press, 1963), p. 200.

17. Cited in Victor Reuther, *The Brothers Reuther and the Story of the UAW: A Memoir* (Boston: Houghton-Mifflin, 1976), p. 420.

18. Cited in Laura McClure, "AFL-CIO: Points of Light for Poland," *Guardian*, June 6, 1990.

19. Ibid.

20. The shift of jobs from Watsonville to Irapuato began in 1983, when Pillsbury-Green Giant first opened its *maquiladora* (export-oriented assembly plant) in the Mexican town. Employment at the Watsonville plant is down from 1300 employees in 1983 to about 100 in 1992. Some 300 of those jobs were lost in the 1991 relocation. Interview with Mike Kostyal, boycott coordinator for *Trabajadores Desplazados*, February 25, 1992.

21. Unidentified worker quoted in a flyer on the "Boycott Pillsbury-Green Giant" campaign, *Trabajadores Desplazados*, June 15, 1991.

22. Interview with Mike Kostyal, February 25, 1992, op. cit.

23. International forces and government insolvency are only partial explanations for the dismal conditions experienced by labor in many countries. Class, gender, and race relationships within a given country are equally important when explaining exploitation and oppression. Mansour Farhang discusses the complicity of third world elites in maintaining a "transnational system of privilege" because of the domestic political and economic benefits they receive in exchange for their cooperation with TNCs and the governments of the developed world. Mansour Farhang, *U.S. Imperialism: The Spanish-American War to the Iranian Revolution* (Boston: South End Press, 1981).

24. A. Sivanandan, "The Global Market Place," *International Labour Reports*, No. 36, November-December 1989, p. 9.

25. Testimony of William C. Doherty, Jr., House Committee on Foreign Affairs, *Foreign Assistance Act of 1967, Part 5*, 90th Congress, 1st session, May 8-11, 1967, p. 1096.

26. Quoted in Penny Lernoux, *Cry of the People* (Garden City, NY: Doubleday and Co., 1980), p. 211.

27. Top AFL leaders—including Samuel Gompers, John Mitchell of the United Mine Workers, and Daniel J. Keefe of the International Longshoremen, Marine and Transport Workers' Union—had already established a precedent for labor-business coalitions of the type Rockefeller put together. These and other labor officials served on the National Civic Federation (NCF) with key members of the U.S. industrialist and financial elite. Established in 1900, the NCF was a tripartite body that aimed to reduce conflict between employers and workers in the capitalist economy. In exchange for giving up radical demands and for supporting the capitalist system, the unions represented in the NCF won recognition of their organizations and obtained other material benefits. Among the employers represented on the body were such notorious union-busters as Mark Hanna, J. Ogden Armour (whose workers were described as "white slaves" by an AFL investigating committee), and Cyrus H. McCormick. The follow-

ing authors discuss the NCF and official labor's collaboration with representatives of U.S. monopoly capitalism during the early years of the twentieth century: Gordon M. Jensen, "The National Civic Federation: American Business in an Age of Social Change and Social Reform, 1900-1910" (Ph.D. dissertation, Princeton University, 1956); Foner, *U.S. Labor Movement and Latin America*, op. cit., pp. 34, 49-50; Philip S. Foner, *History of the Labor Movement in the United States, Vol. 3, The Policies and Practices of the American Federation of Labor, 1900-1909* (New York: International Publishers, 1964), pp. 65-110; and James Weinstein, *The Corporate Ideal in the Liberal State, 1900-1918* (Boston: Beacon Press, 1968).

28. Some of the other corporations which supported AIFLD financially, in addition to those already mentioned, which were represented on its board of directors, included Exxon and Shell oil companies, IBM, Koppers, and Gillette.

29. Cited in Lernoux, *Cry of the People*, op. cit., pp. 226-227.

30. "Amazing Grace," NACLA's *Latin American and Empire Report*, Vol. X, No. 3, March 1976, p. 25.

31. Quoted in *AIFLD Report*, Vol. 19, No. 3, 1981, p. 3.

32. See, for example, Busch, *The Political Role of International Trades Unions*, op. cit.

33. The critical position eventually taken by the U.S. federation on the Pinochet dictatorship was particularly ironic because of the participation of AIFLD-backed unions in bringing down the democratically elected government of Salvador Allende and the part played by ITT, represented on the institute's board, in the 1973 coup.

34. The quotation is from the Democracy Program, *The Commitment to Democracy: A Bipartisan Approach* (Washington: American Political Foundation, undated), p. 46. The Democracy Program study recommended the establishment of the National Endowment for Democracy as part of the task of restoring bipartisanship to U.S. international affairs. The endowment is now one of the biggest funders of the AFL-CIO's international institutes.

Some readers may be skeptical of, or unfamiliar with, this interpretation of the history of U.S. globalism. However, for those who are willing to consider seriously the merits of this analysis, many well-documented books have been written on the subject, including Noam Chomsky, *Turning the Tide: U.S. Intervention in Central America and the Struggle for Peace* (Boston: South End Press, 1985); Farhang, *U.S. Imperialism*, op. cit.; Foner, *U.S. Labor Movement and Latin America*, op. cit.; and Joseph Gerson and Bruce Birchard, eds., *The Sun Never Sets: Confronting the Network of Foreign U.S. Military Bases* (Boston: South End Press, 1991). For a less radical view, see Gardner, *Imperial America*, op. cit.

35. The complicated and varied responses of U.S. labor organizations to U.S. expansionism from 1846 to 1919 are described in Foner, *U.S. Labor Movement and Latin America*, op. cit.

36. See Cantor and Schor, *Tunnel Vision*, op. cit.; and W.M. Scammell, *The International Economy Since 1945* (New York: St. Martin's Press, 1980).

37. See, for example, the Democracy Program study's rationale for increased U.S. activity in global affairs. *The Commitment to Democracy*, op. cit.

38. Enid Eckstein, "What Is the AFL-CIO Doing in the Philippines?" *Labor Notes*, July 1986.

39. Ibid.

40. Kim Scipes, "Aquino's Total War and the KMU," *Z Magazine*, January 1990, pp. 116-121; and Adele Oltman and Dennis Bernstein, "Counterinsurgency in the Philippines," *Covert Action Information Bulletin*, No. 29, Winter 1988.

41. Interview with Michael Bedford, *Third World Reports*, July 18, 1990.

42. Eckstein, *Labor Notes*, op. cit.

43. Scipes, *Z Magazine*, op. cit., p. 119.

44. Carl Gershman, *The Foreign Policy of American Labor*, The Washington Papers, Vol. 3, No. 29 (Beverly Hills, CA: Sage Publications, 1975), p. 66.

45. Ibid.

46. Ibid., p. 4.

47. See Sidney Lens, "Labor Lieutenants and the Cold War," in Burton Hall, ed., *Autocracy and Insurgency in Organized Labor* (New Brunswick, NJ: Transaction Books, 1972); and Cantor and Schor, *Tunnel Vision*, op. cit.

48. The quote is from Edwin Lahey of Knight Press, cited in Lens, ibid., p. 314.

49. Quoted in ibid., p. 315.

50. Ibid., p. 312.

51. This analysis was drawn from an interview with Irving Brown conducted by Sidney Lens and described in ibid.

52. This top unionist in the international affairs department of a major U.S. union requested to remain anonymous.

53. Cantor and Schor, *Tunnel Vision*, op. cit., p. 49.

54. Quoted in Senate Committee on Foreign Relations, *Survey of the Alliance for Progress: Labor Policies and Programs*, 90th Congress, 2nd Session, July 15, 1968, p. 11.

55. Cantor and Schor, *Tunnel Vision*, op. cit., p. 32.

56. An excellent and sensitive look at the anticommunism of the United States following World War II is given in Sidney Lens, *The Futile Crusade: Anti-Communism as American Credo* (Chicago: Quadrangle Books, 1964). See also Michael Parenti, *The Anti-Communist Impulse* (New York: Random House, 1969).

57. Gershman, *The Foreign Policy of American Labor*, op. cit., p. 73.

58. For three areas on which the AFL-CIO claims to be in disagreement with Washington, see Hobart A. Spalding, "United States Labor Policy Towards Latin America," unpublished manuscript.

59. To complicate matters more, there is some discrepancy among the different institutes of the AFL-CIO regarding their stands on protectionist legislation. The Asian institute, for example, is more protectionist in its general policy preferences than is the Latin American institute. The explanation in this case appears to be political. AIFLD is more likely to advocate that a given country be given a favorable or unfavorable trade status with the United States on the basis of that government's relationship with Washington.

Chapter 1

1. Interview with Peter Accolla, Latin American/Caribbean Area Adviser, U.S. Department of Labor, January 4, 1991.

2. The AFL-CIO, for instance, funds its "impact projects" (one-time, low-cost social programs) from its own contributions, maintained in accounts separate from government grants and contracts. Figures obtained from *Perspectives on Labor and the World: The AFL-CIO Abroad*, AFL-CIO Publication No. 182 (Washington: AFL-CIO, August 1987), p. 16.

3. Figures given in Spalding, *Trade Unions and the New Industrialization of the Third World*, op. cit., p. 264.

4. Peter M. Cody, Salvador Jimenez, and Dennis H. Wood, DEVRES, INC., "Draft Report of an Evaluation of the American Institute for Free Labor Development Program," submitted to AID, December 1986.

5. Report of American Voluntary Agencies Engaged in Overseas Relief and Development Registered with the Agency for International Development, Bureau for Food for Peace and Voluntary Assistance, *Voluntary Foreign Aid Programs 1983-1984* (Washington: AID, 1984).

6. Interview with Harry Wing, Office of Private and Voluntary Cooperation, AID, December 27, 1990.

7. Interview with Richard Whitaker, Bureau for Asia and Private Enterprise, AID, January 4, 1991.

8. Democracy Initiatives information obtained from AID, "FY 1990

Democracy Initiatives and Human Rights Program Summary" (Washington: AID, 1990); and Interview with Travis Horel, Policy Office, AID, January 4, 1991. At various times, AID has also provided funding for AIFLD-administered revolving loan funds to finance economic and social development projects. These have included the Regional Revolving Loan Fund ($625,000 in 1968, plus later contributions of $2,154,274), the Caribbean Basin Loan Fund ($387,000 in 1979), the Agrarian Union Development Department Revolving Fund ($150,000 in 1979), and the Eastern Caribbean Revolving Loan Fund ($333,000 in 1980). For figures on AID contributions to AIFLD loan funds, see Cody et al., "Draft Report," op. cit., p. 27.

9. Interview with Jack Francis, Latin America and Caribbean Office, AID, January 24, 1991.

10. Figures obtained from *The AFL-CIO Abroad*, op. cit., pp. 11-15.

11. Interview with Richard Whitaker, January 4, 1991, op. cit.

12. "FY 1990 Democracy Initiatives and Human Rights Program Summary," op. cit.

13. Interview with Travis Horel, January 4, 1991, op. cit.

14. AID, "FY 1990 Democracy Initiatives and Human Rights Program Summary," op. cit.

15. "No Trade Union Imperialism," *International Labour Reports*, May/June 1985.

16. The AID funds originated in two congressional initiatives, the "Urgent Assistance for Democracy in Panama Act of 1990," and the "Support for Eastern European Democracy (SEED) Act," and were channeled through NED. See National Endowment for Democracy board meeting minutes, January 19, 1990 and March 29, 1990.

17. Statement of Joan M. McCabe, Subcommittee on International Operations of the House Committee on Foreign Affairs, *Oversight of the National Endowment for Democracy*, 99th Congress, 2nd session, May 14 and 20, June 11, 1986, p.14.

18. African-American Labor Center, *1988 Annual Report*, AID Grant No. AFR-0441-A-00-5017-00, March 31, 1989, p. 27.

19. Spalding, *Trade Unions and the New Industrialization of the Third World*, op. cit., p. 275.

20. Cited in Hobart Spalding, "Unions Look South," *NACLA Report on the Americas*, May/June 1988, p. 14.

21. An important reference on Haitian labor is Lance Compa, *Labor Rights in Haiti* (Washington: International Labor Rights Education and Research Fund, May 1989). On general economic and political conditions in Haiti, see Amy Wilentz, *The Rainy Season: Haiti Since Duvalier* (New York:

Simon and Schuster, 1989).

22. AALC, *1988 Annual Report,* op. cit., p. 3.

23. Cody et al., "Draft Report," op. cit., p. 22.

24. Asian-American Free Labor Institute, "AAFLI: Questions and Answers," undated informational summary.

25. This congressional staff person requested anonymity.

26. The U.S. Information Agency presumably conducts some type of oversight of its grants for AFL-CIO projects overseas as well. However, Gloria Treyes of USIA's Contracts Division informed this author that answers to questions about the agency's grants with the labor institutes, including funding amounts, types of projects included in the contracts, and so on, would have to be sought through a Freedom of Information Act request and not over the phone. As of this writing, that information is not yet available. Interview with Gloria Treyes, Contracts Division, USIA, February 13, 1991.

27. Senate Committee on Foreign Relations, *Survey of the Alliance for Progress,* op. cit., p. 36.

28. For a detailed look at problems associated with the oversight process and overall accountability at NED, see Beth Sims, *National Endowment for Democracy: A Foreign Policy Branch Gone Awry* (Albuquerque, NM: Inter-Hemispheric Education Resource Center, 1990).

29. Cody et al., "Draft Report," op. cit., p. 2.

30. Interview with Jack Francis, January 24, 1991, op. cit.

31. Interview with Richard Whitaker, January 23, 1991.

32. Cited in John Kelly, "CIA Manipulation of Elections in the Third World," *AfricaAsia,* August/September 1984.

33. Cody et al., "Draft Report," op. cit., p. 22.

34. Interview with Richard Whitaker, January 23, 1991, op. cit.

35. Ibid.

36. Cody et al., "Draft Report," op. cit., p. 23.

37. Ibid.

38. Interview with Richard Whitaker, January 23, 1991, op. cit.

39. Letter from Timothy Ryan, AAFLI, May 3, 1990.

40. Telecon record of conversation between Tresa Bass, NED, and Anne Knipper, FTUI, May 9, 1989.

41. Undated memorandum from Eugenia Kemble to Carl Gershman, "Budget List Enclosed," reproduced in Carol L. Somplatsky-Jarman, *Report on the National Endowment for Democracy and Free Trade Union*

Institute, AFL-CIO (New York: National Committee on Religion and Labor, 1986).

42. Phil Bronstein and David Johnston, "U.S. Funding Anti-Left Fight in Philippines," *San Francisco Examiner,* July 21, 1985.

43. Until 1981, AIFLD was the only exception to this rule. As noted previously, the institute included on its board of trustees representatives of large U.S. corporations with interests in Latin America, as well as labor leaders and other functionaries from Latin America.

44. For a discussion of the role of the executive and regional offices in relation to AIFLD, see Cody et al., "Draft Report," op. cit., pp. 11-13.

45. This staff person asked to remain anonymous.

46. Cody et al., "Draft Report," op. cit., p. 12.

47. Ibid.

48. This information is derived from conversations with individuals who occupied top staff positions in the international affairs departments of major U.S. unions.

49. *The AFL-CIO Abroad,* op. cit.

50. The following authors examine Gompers' influence on the international activities of the AFL and his own philosophy regarding labor internationalism: Gershman, *The Foreign Policy of American Labor,* op. cit.; Kim Scipes, "Trade Union Imperialism in the U.S. Yesterday: Business Unionism, Samuel Gompers and AFL Foreign Policy," *Newsletter of International Labour Studies* (The Hague), Nos. 40-41, January-April, 1989, pp. 4-20; and Foner, *U.S. Labor Movement and Latin America,* op. cit.

51. Speech to the Saratoga (New York) Conference, August 20, 1898, in the *American Federationist,* Vol. 5, 1898, p. 139.

52. For excellent overviews of organized U.S. labor's early role in U.S. foreign policy, see Foner, *U.S. Labor Movement and Latin America,* op. cit.; and Radosh, *American Labor and United States Foreign Policy,* op. cit.

53. Having begun his career as a socialist, Gompers later turned away from marxist strategies based on class struggle and increasingly emphasized the collaborative approaches and narrow organizing strategies of business unionism. He apparently came to believe that focusing on the limited economistic objectives of *trade unions,* not on workers as a *class,* would result in real gains in power for the working class. His growing conservatism also included acceptance of the general framework of the U.S. political and economic system. For more on this transition, see Scipes, "Trade Union Imperialism in the U.S. Yesterday," op. cit.; and Foner, *History of the Labor Movement in the United States, Vol. 3,* op. cit., especially the chapter on "Business Unionism."

54. Henry W. Berger, "Labor and State: Marriage of Convenience," *The*

Nation, January 13, 1969, p. 47; and Foner, *U.S. Labor Movement and Latin America,* op. cit., pp. 176-177.

55. The founding of the Pan-American Federation of Labor is described by Foner, *U.S. Labor Movement and Latin America,* ibid., pp. 172-180.

56. Santiago Iglesias, "Pan-American Federation of Labor: Creation of A. F. of L.," *International Molders' Journal,* July 1927, pp. 390-392.

57. See Jonathan Kwitny, *Endless Enemies: The Making of an Unfriendly World* (New York: Congdon & Weed, 1984); and Cantor and Schor, *Tunnel Vision,* op. cit.

58. For more on these individuals, see the article by Sidney Lens, "Labor Lieutenants and the Cold War, in *Autocracy and Insurgency in Organized Labor,* op. cit. This article gives a quick rundown on many of the individuals who participated in the AFL's postwar battle for European unions.

59. See, for example, Kwitny, *Endless Enemies,* op. cit., pp. 339-341.

60. Ibid., p. 340.

61. Cantor and Schor, *Tunnel Vision,* op. cit., pp. 35-37.

62. Busch, *The Political Role of International Trades Unions,* op. cit., p. 89.

63. See the chapter on "The Development of African Unionism" in Busch, *The Political Role of International Trades Unions,* ibid.

64. Ibid.

65. See, for example, ibid.; Nathan Godfried, "Spreading American Corporatism: Trade Union Education for Third World Labour," *Review of African Political Economy,* September 1987; and Paul Tiyambe Zeleza, "Trade Union Imperialism: American Labour, the ICFTU, and the Kenyan Labour Movement," *Social and Economic Studies,* Vol. 36, No. 2, 1987.

66. Lenny Siegel, "Asian Labor: The American Connection," *Pacific Research & World Empire Telegram,* July/August 1975.

67. Ibid., pp. 4 and 6.

68. Moving into the 1990s, ORIT appears to be distancing itself from its northern counterpart, arguing in its last convention that class considerations could not be excluded from an analysis of labor conditions in Latin America. Although still a recipient of AFL-CIO funding, philosophically ORIT moved more in line with European Social and Christian Democratic unions. See ORIT, *Desafío del Cambio: Nuevos Rumbos del Sindicalismo* (Caracas, Venezuela: Nueva Sociedad, 1989).

Chapter 2

1. Quoted in Jonas Bernstein, "Activism Is Part of AFL-CIO Work," *Insight,* May 30, 1988.

2. Lane Kirkland, "Promoting Democracy: Labor's Enduring Commitment," *Commonsense,* Vol. 6, December 1983, p. 107.

3. Bill Brock, "The Democracy Program: A Strong Foundation," *Commonsense,* Vol. 6, December 1983, p. 91. Brock was the chairman of the American Political Foundation's Democracy Program, which recommended that Congress establish NED. He became chairman of NED in 1988. A leading figure in the U.S. Republican Party, Brock served as chairman of the Republican National Committee from 1977 to 1980. Under President Reagan, Brock acted as U.S. Trade Representative, a cabinet-level position, from 1981 to 1985. He became Reagan's Secretary of Labor in 1985, a position he held until 1987.

4. Christopher Madison, "Selling Democracy," *National Journal,* June 28, 1986.

5. Cody et al., "Draft Report," op. cit., p. 6.

6. Busch, *The Political Role of International Trades Unions,* op. cit.

7. Roy Godson, "Labor's Role in Building Democracy," in Ralph M. Goldman and William A. Douglas, eds., *Promoting Democracy: Opportunities and Issues* (New York: Praeger, 1988).

8. Chuck Sudetic, "Bulgarian Premier Quits After Two Weeks of Protest," *New York Times,* November 30, 1990. The AID and USIA funds were funneled through the National Endowment for Democracy to the Free Trade Union Institute and the AFL-CIO itself. For information on these grants and the AFL-CIO's support for Podkrepa, see *The Bulletin,* AFL-CIO Department of International Affairs, March 1990; and Board Meeting Minutes of the National Endowment for Democracy, March 29, 1990 and June 8, 1990. In keeping with NED's strategy of targeting various sectors in a society for political mobilization, other 1990 NED grants for Bulgarian opposition organizations were channeled through U.S. organizations such as the National Democratic Institute for International Affairs, National Republican Institute for International Affairs, Institute for Democracy in Eastern Europe, International Foundation for Electoral Systems, and Freedom House. The grants assisted political parties, unionists, students, an opposition newspaper, and various civic groups. They paid for visitor exchanges, technical assistance, equipment purchases, pre-election activities, training, media efforts, and institution-building.

9. See, for example, Michael Massing, "Trotsky's Orphans: From Bolshevism to Reaganism," *The New Republic,* June 22, 1987; and "The Neocon Family Tree," *Mother Jones,* July/August 1986.

10. Jack Clark, "The 'Ex' Syndrome," *NACLA Report on the Americas,* May/June 1988, p. 26.

11. The "old boy" network and conflict-of-interest structure built into the NED system are exemplified by this grant to the American Federation of Teachers. At the time, the AFT's Albert Shanker was a member of the board

of the National Endowment for Democracy, which awarded this grant. Shanker is also on the board of trustees of Freedom House. Eugenia Kemble of the Free Trade Union Institute—the pass-through for the grant from NED to the teachers' union—was formerly Shanker's assistant at the AFT. Her brother, Penn Kemble, is a senior associate at Freedom House. Tom Kahn, also of the AFT, links the labor federation's international affairs department to the grant. Like Shanker, the Kembles, and Kahn, Eric Chenowith—who wrote the article which appeared in the Freedom House journal, *Freedom at Issue*—is a member of Social Democrats USA.

12. See the interesting background piece by Michael Massing on Penn Kemble and the other "Gang of Four" members, Bruce Cameron, Robert Leiken, and Bernard Aronson. Michael Massing, "Contra Aides," *Mother Jones*, October 1987.

13. For information on the CIA-related activities of the International Rescue Committee, see Christopher Simpson, *Blowback* (New York: Weidenfelt & Nicolson, 1988); Steve Weissman, *The Trojan Horse: A Radical Look at Foreign Aid* (San Francisco: Ramparts Press, 1974); Russ Bellant, *Old Nazis, The New Right and the Reagan Administration* (Cambridge, MA: Political Research Associates, 1989); and Robert Scheer and Warren Hinckle, "The Vietnam Lobby," *Ramparts,* July 1965.

14. *AAFLI News*, Vol. 21, No. 4, August 1990.

15. Quoted in Sidney Blumenthal, "Pro-Contra Group Gives Tour of Bases," *Washington Post,* August 8, 1986.

16. Ibid.

17. Ellen Ray, William Schaap, Karl Van Meter, and Louis Wolf, *Dirty Work: The CIA in Africa* (Seacaucus NJ: Lyle Stuart, Inc., 1979).

18. National Endowment for Democracy Annual Report, 1985.

19. Information for this profile on Doherty was drawn from a number of sources, including Philip Agee, *Inside the Company: CIA Diary* (New York: Stonehill, 1975); Kwitny, *Endless Enemies,* op. cit.; Al Weinrub and William Bollinger, *The AFL-CIO in Central America* (Oakland, CA: Labor Network on Central America, 1987); Howard Frazier, ed., *Uncloaking the CIA* (New York: The Free Press, 1978); Walter Poelchau, ed., *White Paper Whitewash: Interviews with Philip Agee on the CIA and El Salvador* (New York: Deep Cover Books, 1981); and Raymond Bonner, *Weakness and Deceit: U.S. Policy and El Salvador* (New York: Times Books, 1984).

20. Kwitny, *Endless Enemies,* op. cit., pp. 346-347.

21. Agee, *Inside the Company,* op. cit., p. 607.

22. Donald Robinson, "Bill Doherty's Blue Collar Freedom Fighters," *Reader's Digest,* September 1985; and Spalding, *Trade Unions and the New Industrialization of the Third World,* op. cit., p. 275.

23. U.S. Government Interagency Team on Commercial and Private Sector

Initiatives, "Prospects for Growth in Grenada: The Role of the Private Sector," (Washington: December 5, 1983), pp. iii-iv and 20-21.

24. Cited in Lernoux, *Cry of the People,* op. cit., p. 212.

Chapter 3

1. Agee, *Inside the Company,* op. cit., p. 601.

2. Senate Committee on Foreign Relations, *Survey of the Alliance for Progress,* op. cit., p. 9.

3. Kwitny, *Endless Enemies,* op. cit.

4. Ibid., p. 341.

5. Until recently AIFLD-trained unionists were thought to have had a major role in the overthrow of the Brazilian government of João Goulart in 1964. This belief was founded in part on revelations that AIFLD trainings of Brazilian unionists had skyrocketed during the months preceding the coup. More significantly, William Doherty boasted to Congress of Brazilian labor's role in the coup, saying that AIFLD-trained graduates "were so active that they became intimately involved in some of the clandestine operations of the revolution . . . Many of the trade union leaders—some of whom were actually trained in our Institute—were involved in the revolution, and in the overthrow of the Goulart regime." William Doherty, in panel discussion, Mutual Broadcasting System, July 12, 1964. Quoted in Senate Committee on Foreign Relations, *Survey of the Alliance for Progress,* op. cit. New research, however, has shown no significant role in the coup played by either AIFLD or its trainees. See Ruth Leacock, *Requiem for Revolution* (Kent, OH: Kent State University Press, 1990) for the newest research on this topic. On the other hand, Kwitny presents information that contradicts Leacock's. Ibid., pp. 348-349.

6. This slip occurred in 1981 at the U.S. Supreme Court hearing of Philip Agee. Agee, a former CIA operative, was challenging the government's decision to revoke his passport in response to the revelations he made of CIA activities in his book *Inside the Company.* The U.S. solicitor general, Wade H. McCree, Jr., arguing for the government, used the example of Hammer and Pearlman to bolster his case that Agee would use his passport to publicize important government secrets, such as the identity of CIA agents. Kwitny, ibid., p. 348.

7. For information on Brown's CIA activities, see ibid., pp. 344-346; Agee, *Inside the Company,* op. cit., pp. 75 and 604; and Weinrub and Bollinger, *The AFL-CIO in Central America,* op. cit., p. 7.

8. Godfried, *Review of African Political Economy,* op. cit., p. 56.

9. Interview with Kenneth Mokoena, National Security Archive, December 24, 1990.

10. Kwitny, *Endless Enemies,* op. cit., p. 345.

11. Ibid., p. 346.

12. Prexy Nesbitt and Don Will, "AFL-CIO in Africa—A Damning Indictment," *Guardian Labor Supplement,* Fall 1986.

13. See, for example, the chapter on "The Development of African Unionism" in Busch, *The Political Role of International Trades Unions,* op. cit.

14. Zeleza, *Social and Economic Studies,* op. cit.

15. For examples and discussion, see ibid.; Godfried, *Review of African Political Economy,* op. cit.; Anne Newman, "Is American Support Dividing South African Labor?" *Africa News,* June 2, 1986; Andy Weir, "Africa Divides: African Unity Collapses with a Shove from the U.S.," *International Labour Reports,* May/June 1986; Andy Weir, "How the U.S. Tries to Buy African Unions," *International Labour Reports,* May/June 1986; Ronaldo Munck, *The New International Labour Studies: An Introduction* (London: Zed Books Ltd, 1988), p. 192; and American Labor Education Center, "Which Side Are You On?" *American Labor,* No. 27.

16. Cited in Weir, "How the U.S. Tries to Buy African Unions, *International Labour Reports,* ibid.

17. Ibid., p. 22.

18. Cited in Spooner, *Partners or Predators,* op. cit., p. 34.

19. Agee, *Inside the Company,* op. cit., p. 616.

20. Ibid., p. 618.

21. Siegel, *Pacific Research & World Empire Telegram,* op. cit., p. 3.

22. David Robie, *Blood on Their Banner: Nationalist Struggles in the South Pacific* (London: Zed, 1989), p. 192.

23. Spooner, *Partners or Predators,* op. cit., p. 56.

24. Ibid., p. 57.

25. Ibid., p.13; and Grant No. ANE-0263-G-SS-7028-04, Amendment No. 4, between AAFLI and AID, April 1, 1989.

26. Quoted in Rachael Kamel, *The Global Factory: Analysis and Action for a New Economic Era* (United States: American Friends Service Committee/Omega Press, 1990), p. 56.

27. See Spooner, *Partners or Predators,* op. cit., pp. 12-18; Paul Jenkins, "Raising the Curtain," *International Labour Reports,* No. 40, July/August 1990; and Denis MacShane, "Eastern Promise?" *International Labour Reports,* No. 40, July/August 1990.

28. *The AFL-CIO Abroad,* op. cit., p. 17.

29. For a discussion of the founding of the ILO and its anti-radical objectives, see Radosh, *American Labor and United States Policy,* op. cit., pp. 268-303.

30. Spalding, "United States Labor Policy Towards Latin America," op. cit., p. 24.

31. Gershman, *The Foreign Policy of American Labor*, op. cit., p. 50.

32. AFL-CIO, *Report to the 1989 Convention from the AFL-CIO Executive Council* (Washington: AFL-CIO, 1989), pp. 261-262.

33. Munck, *The New International Labour Studies*, op. cit., p. 192.

34. Ibid.

35. Quoted in Spooner, *Partners or Predators*, op. cit., p. 52.

36. Munck, *The New International Labour Studies*, op. cit., p. 193.

37. See the description of the International Trade Secretariats and their impact in Asia in Spooner, *Partners or Predators*, op. cit., pp. 19-30.

Chapter 4

1. See descriptions given in AFL-CIO, *Report to the 1989 Convention*, op. cit.; American Institute for Free Labor Development, *AIFLD: Twenty-Five Years of Solidarity with Latin American Workers* (Washington: AIFLD, 1987); American Institute for Free Labor Development, "Annual Progress Report 1962-1989" (Washington: AIFLD, undated); and Spalding, *Trade Unions and the New Industrialization of the Third World*, op. cit., p. 265.

2. Hobart A. Spalding Jr., "AIFLD Amok," *NACLA Report on the Americas*, May/June 1988, p. 21.

3. Interview with Kenneth Mokoena, December 24, 1990, op. cit.

4. Godfried, *Review of African Political Economy*, op. cit., p. 53.

5. Quoted in ibid.

6. AIFLD, "Annual Progress Report 1962-1989," op. cit.

7. AFL-CIO, *Report to the 1989 Convention*, op. cit., p. 265.

8. AAFLI Grant No. ANE-0263-G-SS-7028-04, Amendment No. 4, op. cit., p. 105.

9. Spalding, *Trade Unions and the New Industrialization of the Third World*, op. cit., p. 275.

10. Quoted in Jane Slaughter, "Guatemala: Thanks to You Guys," *International Labour Reports*, May-June 1987, p. 11.

11. See Joe Freeman, "'Minju' Unions Unite," *International Labour Reports*, No. 38, March/April 1990; Joe Freeman, "Testing Times for Korean Union Centre," *International Labour Reports*, No. 40, July/August 1990; "Korea's New Unions Unite," *International Labour Reports*, No. 36, November/December 1989, pp. 4-5; and Asian-American Free Labor Institute, *Annual Report to AID January 1, 1989 to December 31, 1989*, June 30, 1990.

12. The aims of the Korean Trade Union Congress were quoted in Freeman, "'Minju' Unions Unite," *International Labour Reports,* ibid.

13. The comment was made by an AAFLI country representative in Seoul in the mid-1980s. "As we've seen in El Salvador," the representative continued, "it's possible for independent unions to develop in an authoritarian setting." Quoted in Tim Shorrock and Kathy Selvaggio, "Which Side Are You On, AAFLI?" *The Nation,* February 15, 1986.

14. Quoted in Barry and Preusch, *AIFLD in Central America,* op. cit., p. 43.

15. Interview with UNC peasant leader by Tom Barry, Tegucigalpa, Honduras, August 1984.

16. AIFLD, "Annual Progress Report 1962-1989," op. cit.

17. See Barry and Preusch, *AIFLD in Central America,* op. cit., especially pp. 25-29.

18. U.S. Labor Lawyers' Delegation to Nicaragua, *Are Nicaragua's Trade Unions Free?: A Response to the American Institute for Free Labor Development (AIFLD) Report, "Nicaragua, A Revolution Betrayed: Free Labor Persecuted"* (New York: National Lawyers Guild, April 1985), p. 58. Also see the discussion on "Ties Between the CTN, CUS, and the Contras" in the same document, pp. 18-22.

19. Cleto Di Giovanni, "U.S. Policy and the Marxist Threat to Central America," Heritage Foundation, *Backgrounder,* October 15, 1980.

20. For more on these issues, see Spalding, *Trade Unions and the New Industrialization of the Third World,* op. cit.; Carolyn Forché and Philip Wheaton, *History and Motivations of U.S. Involvement in the Control of the Peasant Movement in El Salvador: The Role of AIFLD in the Agrarian Reform Process, 1970-1980* (Washington: EPICA, 1980); and Philip Wheaton, *Agrarian Reform in El Salvador: A Program of Rural Pacification* (Washington: EPICA, 1980).

21. From a study quoted in Frank Arnold, "Ban AIFLD in El Salvador," *Counterspy,* Vol. 4, No. 1, 1980-1981, p. 50.

22. National Labor Committee in Support of Democracy and Human Rights in El Salvador, *El Salvador: Labor, Terror and Peace: A Special Fact Finding Report* (New York: National Labor Committee, 1983), pp. 7-11.

23. This analysis comes from Hilarion Henares of the *Philippine Daily Inquirer,* as interviewed by Adele Oltman and Dennis Bernstein and cited in their article, "Counterinsurgency in the Philippines," *Covert Action Information Bulletin,* No. 29, Winter 1988.

24. Bronstein and Johnston, *San Francisco Examiner,* op. cit.

25. AAFLI Grant No. ANE-0263-G-SS-7028-04, Amendment No. 4, op. cit., p. 5.

26. African-American Labor Center, *1988 Annual Report,* Grant No. AFR-

0441-A-00-5017-00, March 31, 1989.

27. Ibid.

28. African-American Labor Center *1989 Annual Report (January 1 to December 31, 1989)*, AID Grant No. AFR-0441-A-00-5017-00, March 1990.

29. Free Trade Union Institute, "Evaluations of Current Projects," submitted to NED March 5, 1986, p. 53.

30. Ibid., p. 55.

31. William Doherty, Nicaragua, *A Revolution Betrayed: Free Labor Persecuted* (Washington: AIFLD, 1983).

32. U.S. Labor Lawyers' Delegation to Nicaragua, *Are Nicaragua's Trade Unions Free?*, op. cit., p. 6.

33. Washington Area Labor Committee, "Two Tales in Two Cities," *The Labor Link* (Washington DC), Winter 1987.

34. Aaron Bernstein, "Is Big Labor Playing Global Vigilante?" *Business Week*, November 4, 1985.

35. NED document cited in Jack Colhoun, "U.S. Aids Sandinista Rivals to Bolster UNO," *Guardian*, June 6, 1990, p. 9.

36. Confidential Telegram from U.S. Ambassador in Panama to the Secretary of State, "National Endowment for Democracy: Reported Use of Funds to Back Barletta Campaign," No. 021179, April 1984, reproduced in Somplatsky-Jarman, *Report on the National Endowment for Democracy and Free Trade Union Institute, AFL-CIO*, op. cit.

37. Cited in David K. Shipler, "The Role of the United States in an Age of Democratic Revolution," paper presented at conference on "U.S. Electoral Assistance and Democratic Development: Chile, Nicaragua, and Panama," Washington Office on Latin America, January 19, 1990.

38. Ibid.

39. Carol J. Williams, "Hope of U.S. Aid Helped Inspire Bulgaria Revolt," *Los Angeles Times*, December 3, 1990, p. A1. See also Sudetic, *New York Times*, November 30, 1990, op. cit.

40. Quoted in Williams, ibid.

41. The documents were requested by investigative reporter David McKnight of the *Sydney Morning Herald* in Australia. Their contents were first reported in David McKnight, "The CIA's Long History in the Pacific," *Sydney Morning Herald*, May 19, 1987. Cited and discussed in JoAnn Wypijewski, "The Fiji Coup: Was the U.S. Behind It?" *The Nation*, August 15-22, 1987, pp. 117-120.

42. Cited in "AAFLI and the CIA," *Covert Action Information Bulletin*, No. 29, Fall 1987, p. 8.

43. Quoted in Kay Eisenhower, "AFL-CIO Agency Offers Cash to Filipino Union Leader for Vote on U.S. Bases Treaty," *Labor Notes*, No. 152, November 1991.

44. Ibid.

45. Ibid.

46. Reuther was prompted to speak by the AFL-CIO's activities in the Dominican Republic. Quoted in Dan Kurzman, "Lovestone's Cold War: The AFL-CIO Has Its Own CIA," *The New Republic*, June 25, 1966. For more on the AFL-CIO in the Dominican Republic prior to the 1965 U.S. invasion, see Spalding, *Trade Unions and the New Industrialization of the Third World*, op. cit.

47. Weir, "How the U.S. Tries to Buy African Unions," *International Labour Reports*, op. cit.

48. See, for example, Armstrong et al., *Working Against Us*, op. cit.; Robert J. McCartney, "U.S. Cools Support for Duarte," *Washington Post*, March 20, 1985; J. Michael Luhan, "AIFLD's Salvadoran Labor Wars," *Dissent*, Summer 1986; Americas Watch, *Labor Rights in El Salvador* (New York: Americas Watch Committee, 1988); Americas Watch, "Americas Watch Critique of AIFLD Critique on Labor Rights in El Salvador" (New York: Americas Watch Committee, July 5, 1988); and Spalding, "United States Labor Policy Towards Latin America," op. cit. For an alternative view, see David Jessup, "El Salvador Unions—The Real Story," *Dissent*, Fall 1986; and AFL-CIO and AIFLD, "A Critique of the Americas Watch Report on Labor Rights in El Salvador" (Washington: AIFLD, June 10, 1988).

49. Kirkland, *Commonsense*, op. cit., p. 108.

50. Frank Smyth, "Duarte's Secret Friends," *The Nation*, March 14, 1987, pp. 316-318. Also see, Barry and Preusch, *AIFLD in Central America*, op. cit., pp. 31-42. For more recent information on Salvadoran unionism, see National Labor Committee in Support of Democracy and Human Rights in El Salvador, *Worker Rights and the New World Order*, op. cit., pp. 6-25.

51. Quoted in Clifford Krauss, "Labor Activists: Aided by Washington, AFL-CIO Unit Backs Latin Goals of U.S.," *Wall Street Journal*, December 31, 1985.

Chapter 5

1. For discussions of many of these ideas, see Labor Research Association, *Labor Confronts the Transnationals* (New York: International Publishers, 1984); Brecher and Costello, *Z Magazine*, op. cit.; Cantor and Schor, *Tunnel Vision*, op. cit.; Jeremy Brecher and Tim Costello, *Global Village vs. Global Pillage: A One-World Strategy for Labor* (Washington: International Labor Rights Education and Research Fund, 1991); and Stephen Fielding Diamond, "Labor and the North American Free Trade Agreement: Toward a Constructive Critique," paper presented at the Center for U.S.-

Mexican Studies, University of California, San Diego, February 20, 1991.

2. David Montgomery, "Solidarity Across Borders: Making Common Cause," *International Labour Reports,* No. 34/35, July-October 1989, p. 27.

3. The business group is the Salvadoran Foundation for Economic and Social Development (FUSADES). Ad from *Bobbin,* November 1990.

4. Kirkland, *Commonsense,* op. cit., pp. 107-108.

5. There was opposition by mid-level leadership and the rank and file to the AFL-CIO's official foreign policy during the Vietnam War, but this opposition was never translated into serious debates on the convention floor. For the most part, the battle between the AFL-CIO hierarchy and the rank and file over labor's stand in Vietnam took place on the streets and behind closed doors in the federation. In their own conventions, however, individual unions discussed and criticized the war in floor debates. Among the unions that adopted resolutions critical of U.S. prosecution of the war were the United Auto Workers; the Retail, Wholesale and Department Store Union; and the Amalgamated Clothing Workers. As early as 1966, the United Packinghouse Workers Union adopted a resolution declaring that "the basic and urgent objective of our national policy should be to end the war in Vietnam." The resolution also condemned as "unthinking and irresponsible" those people who called for the United States to "bomb cities and civilians, and mine harbors even at the risk of open conflict with other nations." Cited in Philip S. Foner, *U.S. Labor and the Vietnam War* (New York: International Publishers, 1989), pp. 38-39.

6. For more on these historic efforts, see Dave Slaney, "Solidarity and Self-Interest," *NACLA Report on the Americas,* May/June 1988, pp. 28-36; Hobart A. Spalding, "The Two Latin American Foreign Policies of the U.S. Labor Movement: The AFL-CIO vs Rank and File," unpublished manuscript; and Cantor and Schor, *Tunnel Vision,* op. cit.

7. Slaney, ibid., p. 34.

8. Munck, *The New International Labour Studies,* op. cit., p. 194.

9. See National Labor Committee in Support of Democracy and Human Rights in El Salvador, *Worker Rights and the New World Order,* op. cit., for examples from El Salvador, Honduras, and Guatemala.

10. See, for example, Armstrong et al., *Working Against Us,* op. cit.; and Spalding, "United States Labor Policy Towards Latin America," op. cit.

11. Interview with Kenneth Mokoena, December 24, 1990, op. cit.; Interview with Debi Duke, American Labor Education Center, December 27, 1990; and Debi Duke, "Behind the AFL-CIO's Warm Welcome of Mandela: Can a Leopard Change Its Spots," *Labor Notes,* January 1991.

12. Quoted in D. Elson, "Bound Together with One String," *International Labour Reports,* No. 10, July/August 1985, p. 19.

13. Some of the best work available on these progressive union efforts has

been done by Jeremy Brecher and Tim Costello. See their work in *Z Magazine,* op. cit.; and Brecher and Costello, *Global Village vs. Global Pillage,* op. cit. Also see Diamond, "Labor and the North American Free Trade Agreement," op. cit., and Kamel, *The Global Factory,* op. cit., for discussions of networking strategies and suggested components of a progressive labor response to global economic integration.

14. See Richard J. Barnet and Ronald E. Müller, *Global Reach: The Power of the Multinational Corporations* (New York: Simon and Schuster, 1974) for an exploration of the declining role of the nation-state in a world of TNC dominance.

15. Brecher and Costello, *Global Village vs. Global Pillage,* op. cit., p. 3.

16. Ibid., p. 1.

17. See, for example, Joe Uehlein, "Using Labor's Trade Secretariats," *Labor Research Review, Vol. 13, Solidarity Across Borders: U.S. Labor in a Global Economy* (Chicago: Midwest Center for Labor Research, Spring 1989).

18. Ibid.

19. For discussions of such coalitions in the arena of U.S. Central American foreign policy, see Slaney, *NACLA Report on the Americas,* op. cit. Also see Spooner, *Partners or Predators,* op. cit., for a look at such coalitions and their impacts on Asian labor. For discussions that emphasize progressive labor and international solidarity actions, see the pieces by Brecher and Costello, *Z Magazine,* op. cit., and *Global Village vs. Global Pillage,* op. cit.; and the entire issue of *Labor Research Review, Vol. 13, Solidarity Across Borders,* op. cit.

20. See, for example, Portland Labor Committee for Peace in the Middle East, "Blood for Oil: Good for Business? Bad for Labor!" undated pamphlet.

Index

About South End Press

South End Press is a nonprofit, collectively-run book publisher with over 175 titles in print. Since our founding in 1977, we have tried to meet the needs of readers who are exploring, or are already committed to, the politics of radical social change.

Our goal is to publish books that encourage critical thinking and constructive action on the key political, cultural, social, economic, and ecological issues shaping life in the United States and in the world. In this way, we hope to give expression to a wide diversity of democratic social movements and to provide an alternative to the products of corporate publishing.

Through the Institute for Social and Cultural Change, South End Press works with other political media projects—*Z Magazine*; Speak Out!, a speakers bureau; the Publishers Support Project; and the New Liberation News Service—to expand access to information and critical analysis. If you would like a free catalog of South End Press books or information about our membership program—which offers two free books and a 40% discount on all titles—please write to us at South End Press, 116 Saint Botolph Street, Boston, MA 02115.

Other titles of interest from South End Press:

Mask of Democracy
Labor Suppression in Mexico Today
Dan La Botz

Collateral Damage
The New World Order at Home and Abroad
Ed. by Cynthia Peters

Storm Signals
Structural Adjustment and Development Alternatives in the Caribbean
Kathy McAfee

The Coors Connection
How Coors' Family Philanthropy Undermines Democratic Pluralism
Russ Bellant

Sisterhood and Solidarity
Feminism and Labor in Modern Times
Diane Balser